GW00692183

AS Psychology
UNIT 1
2ND EDITION

AQA

Specification
A

Module 1: Cognitive and Developmental Psychology

Cara Flanagan

Philip Allan Updates
Market Place
Deddington
Oxfordshire
OX15 0SE

Orders
Bookpoint Ltd, 130 Milton Park, Abingdon, Oxfordshire, OX14 4SB
tel: 01235 827720
fax: 01235 400454
e-mail: uk.orders@bookpoint.co.uk
Lines are open 9.00 a.m.–5.00 p.m., Monday to Saturday, with a 24-hour
message answering service. You can also order through the Philip Allan
Updates website:
www.philipallan.co.uk

ISBN-13: 978-0-86003-890-0
ISBN-10: 0-86003-890-4

This Guide has been written specifically to support students preparing for the
AQA Specification A AS Psychology Unit 1 examination. The content has been
neither approved nor endorsed by AQA and remains the sole responsibility of
the author.

Printed by MPG Books, Bodmin

Philip Allan Updates' policy is to use papers that are natural, renewable and
recyclable products and made from wood grown in sustainable forests. The
logging and manufacturing processes are expected to conform to the environ-
mental regulations of the country of origin.

Contents

Introduction

■ ■ ■

Content Guidance

■ ■ ■

Questions and Answers

Introduction

About this guide

This is a guide to Unit 1 of AQA(A) AS Psychology, which examines the content of **Module 1: Cognitive and Developmental Psychology**. This guide is intended as a revision *aid*, rather than a textbook or revision guide. Therefore, the emphasis is on *how* the specification content is examined and on showing you how different levels of answer to sample questions will be assessed.

The two compulsory sections of the AQA(A) Cognitive and Developmental Psychology are covered, and for each of these we take you through the following:

- the specification content for each topic. This is fully explained so that you know exactly what you might be asked to demonstrate in an examination.

- appropriate content relevant to those topics. This gives you a minimal coverage of each topic area. This is not intended as the *only* appropriate content for a given topic area, but does give you an idea of how you might present your answer to a question set on this particular aspect of the specification.

- a set of definitions of key terms for each section, vital for those 'What is meant by?' questions. Each of these has been constructed to be succinct but informative and therefore appropriate for such questions.

- *four* sample questions in the style of AQA(A) AS examination questions, together with full explanations of their requirements. These questions demonstrate the typical format of AQA(A) AS questions, as well as the appropriate breakdown of marks between AO1 and AO2 skills (see below).

- a typical 'grade C' student response to each of these questions, together with examiner comments showing where the marks have been gained and lost.

- a 'grade A' response to each of these questions, showing how they might have been answered by a very good student.

How to use this guide

This book is not intended as a set of model answers to examination questions, nor as an account of the *right* material to include should you be asked to display this very same knowledge. It is intended to give you an idea of the way that your examination will be structured and how you might improve your own examination performance.

It is suggested that you read through the relevant section in Content Guidance before attempting a question from the Question and Answer section, and only read the specimen answers after you have tackled the question yourself.

The examination:
AO1 and AO2 questions

Unit 1 is assessed in a *1 hour* examination. Your examination paper will comprise *four questions*, two of which are on Cognitive Psychology and two on Developmental Psychology. You are required to select *one* on Cognitive Psychology and *one* on Developmental Psychology.

Each question is worth *30 marks*. Within each question, there will be *three parts*. The *last part* is always the **AO1 + AO2** part of the assessment, and the preceding parts are purely **AO1**. The **AO1** question parts test your *knowledge* and *understanding* skills, while **AO2** tests your skills of *analysis* and *evaluation*.

Questions

The following are *examples* of the types of question that are used to assess AO1 and AO2.

AO1 questions

What is meant by the terms attachment, deprivation and privation?　　*(2+2+2 marks)*

Describe two differences between secure and insecure attachment.　　*(3+3 marks)*

Describe the aims/procedures/findings/conclusions* of one study of privation.
(6 marks)

[*any combination of two of these aspects of the study]

Outline two explanations of why secure attachments develop.　　*(3+3 marks)*

Describe one explanation of attachment (e.g. Bowlby).　　*(6 marks)*

Give two criticisms of the explanation you have given above.　　*(3+3 marks)*

AO1 + AO2 questions

'One problem with memory research is that it tends to be largely laboratory-based.'
Consider the value of memory research for real-world applications, such as eyewitness testimony.　　*(18 marks)*

Briefly *outline* Bowlby's maternal deprivation hypothesis and *evaluate* the effects of short-term deprivation/separation on subsequent development.　　*(18 marks)*

'Children differ considerably in their attachments to their caregivers. This may be related to differences in child-rearing practices, and child-rearing practices vary from one culture to another.'
To what extent does research demonstrate cross-cultural variations in attachment?
(18 marks)

Effective exam performance

- *Read the questions carefully*, as marks are only available for the specific requirements of the question set. Miss those out and you lose marks; include something irrelevant and you have wasted valuable time.

- Remember that *each mark* is equivalent to approximately *1 minute* of thinking and writing, so it is vital to use this time wisely, neither extending it nor skimping on it.

- *Make a brief plan* before answering the question. This can be in your head or on paper, but you must know where you are going and how long it will take you to get there. *Time management is absolutely vital.*

- Sometimes questions ask you to *outline* something. You need to practise doing this as the skill of précis is not as easy as it looks.

- *Be aware of the difference between AO1 and AO2 questions.* AO2 questions are not just an opportunity for more descriptive content. You must *engage with the question topic* in the required way.

- In AO1 questions, the emphasis is on the *amount* of relevant material presented (e.g. 'limited' or 'basic'), the amount of *detail* given (e.g. 'lacking detail') and the *accuracy* of the material (e.g. 'muddled').

- For the AO2 component of AO1 + AO2 question parts, the emphasis is on the *amount* and *level* of the critical commentary (e.g. 'superficial'), its *thoroughness* (e.g. 'reasonably thorough') and how *effectively* it has been used (e.g. 'highly effective').

How are the marks awarded?

Mark allocations for AO1 2-mark questions

'What is meant by the terms attachment, deprivation and privation?' *(2+2+2 marks)*

Marks	Criteria
2 marks	Accurate and detailed
1 mark	Basic, lacking detail, muddled or flawed
0 marks	Inappropriate or incorrect

Mark allocations for AO1 3- and 6-mark questions

'Outline two explanations for forgetting in short-term memory.' *(3+3 marks)*

'Outline findings of research into the effects of day-care on children's social development.' *(6 marks)*

3-mark questions	6-mark questions	Criteria
3 marks	6–5 marks	Accurate and detailed
2 marks	4–3 marks	Limited, generally accurate but less detailed
1 mark	2–1 marks	Basic, lacking in detail, muddled or flawed
0 marks	0 marks	Inaccurate or irrelevant

Mark allocations for AO2

Certain questions are AO1 + AO2. They are awarded 18 marks: 6 marks AO1 (assessed using the criteria above) and 12 marks AO2, assessed according to the criteria below. The heading 'commentary' applies to the specific AO2 requirement of the question (e.g. 'evaluate' or 'to what extent?').

Marks	Commentary	Analysis	Use of material
12–11	Informed	Reasonably thorough	Effective
10–9	Reasonable	Slightly limited	Effective
8–7	Reasonable	Limited	Reasonably effective
6–5	Basic	Limited	Reasonably effective
4–3	Superficial	Rudimentary	Minimal interpretation
2–1	Just discernible	Weak and muddled	Mainly irrelevant
0	Wholly irrelevant	Wholly irrelevant	Wholly irrelevant

Content
Guidance

In this section, content guidance is offered on the topics of human memory (Cognitive Psychology) and attachments in development (Developmental Psychology).

Each topic begins with an outline and explanation of the AQA Specification A requirement for this part of the module. This is followed by a more detailed look at the theories and studies that make up the module content.

Knowledge of appropriate theories and studies is essential for the AS examination. It is also important to be able to assess the value of these theories and studies, and this is done using regular 'Evaluation' features and criticisms of studies.

At the end of each topic, definitions are provided for key terms — those terms that you might be asked to define in an examination.

Names and publication dates have been given when referring to research studies. The full references for these studies should be available in textbooks should the reader wish to research the topic further.

Cognitive psychology: human memory

Short-term memory and long-term memory

Specification content

Research into the nature and structure of memory, including encoding, capacity and duration of short-term memory (STM) and long-term memory (LTM). The multi-store model of memory (Atkinson and Shiffrin) and alternatives to this including working memory (Baddeley and Hitch) and levels of processing (Craik and Lockhart).

One way to consider human memory is to look at the characteristics of **short-** and **long-term memory**. You are required to distinguish between these memory stores in terms of **encoding** (how the material is stored), **capacity** (how much data can be held in the store) and **duration** (how long the memory lasts).

Three models of memory are named in the specification: **multi-store model**, **working memory** and **levels of processing**. This means that you *must* cover these theories/models. For each one you must be able to describe it and demonstrate your understanding, be familiar with appropriate research evidence, and know the strengths and limitations of the theory/model.

Distinguishing between STM and LTM

The following table summarises the distinctions between STM and LTM:

	Short-term memory		Long-term memory	
Encoding	Acoustic	Baddeley (1966)	Semantic	Baddeley (1966)
Capacity	7 ± 2 chunks of information	Simon (1974)	Unlimited	
Duration	Short (15–30 seconds)	Peterson and Peterson (1959)	Long, potentially forever	Bahrick et al. (1975)
Forgetting	e.g. decay, displacement		e.g. interference, context-dependent	
Brain damage	Anterograde and retrograde amnesia	Shallice and Warrington (1970)		
Serial position effect	Recency effect	Glanzer and Cunitz (1966)	Primacy effect	Glanzer and Cunitz (1966)

One study of encoding in STM and LTM (Baddeley, 1966)

Aims

This aimed to support earlier research that showed that STM was largely based on an acoustic code and find out whether LTM was also acoustically coded. In addition, it explored whether either STM or LTM was semantically coded.

Procedures

Participants were given four sets of words to recall: acoustically similar (e.g. man, cap, can, cab, mad), acoustically dissimilar (e.g. pit, few, cow, pen), semantically similar (e.g. great, large, big, huge), and semantically dissimilar (e.g. good, huge, hot, safe). One group of participants was asked to recall the words immediately (STM), whereas another group was asked to recall the words after an interval of 20 minutes (LTM).

Findings

If participants were asked to recall the word list immediately (STM) they did less well with acoustically similar words than with acoustically dissimilar words. When they recalled the words after an interval (LTM), they performed the same on the acoustic lists but there were differences on the semantic lists.

Conclusions

This suggests that STM is based largely on an acoustic code, whereas LTM tends to be based on semantic codes.

Criticisms

Laboratory experiments are well controlled and permit identification of cause-and-effect relationships (high internal validity). On the other hand, they tend to involve explicit (conscious recall) rather than implicit memory, and declarative memory (memory for things) rather than procedural memory (memory for how to do things). Therefore, they may apply only to limited aspects of memory (low external validity).

One study of capacity in STM (Simon, 1974)

Aims

Miller (1956) demonstrated that the span of STM is not limited by bits of information, but is proportional to the number of chunks, suggesting that the capacity of STM is 7±2 chunks. Simon wondered whether this 'constant capacity in chunks' hypothesis was true no matter what the chunk size.

Procedures

Simon tried memorising different kinds of items: words with one, two and three syllables; and another selection of words (Lincoln, milky, criminal, differential, address, way, lawyer, calculus, Gettysburg). He then rearranged these into: Lincoln's Gettysburg address; milky way, criminal lawyer and differential calculus. Finally, he tried to learn: four score and seven years ago; to be or not to be, that is the question; in the beginning was the word; all's fair in love and war.

Findings

Simon found that he could recall about seven one- and two-syllable words and six three-syllable words. He found he could not remember all the words Lincoln through to Gettysburg, but he could remember these words in meaningful phrases. However, he could only recall three of the longer phrases.

Conclusions

This highlights the difficulty in identifying what a chunk is. One syllable is not a chunk — he could remember six chunks and 12 chunks (two-syllable words) as easily. In some situations, a phrase can be a chunk — he could remember 'criminal lawyer' more easily than those words separately. However, when the 'chunk' became too long (e.g. all's fair in love and war), this placed an extra load on memory. We can conclude that the number of chunks alone is not the only constraint on memory and that size of chunk (and time taken to learn) affects recall.

Criticisms

The methodology was not highly controlled and the study concerned only one aspect of memory.

One study of this duration in STM (Peterson and Peterson, 1959)

Aims

This investigated how long material is retained in STM when verbal rehearsal is prevented.

Procedures

Participants were shown trigrams (e.g. CTG) and asked to recall them after 3, 6, 9, 12, 15 or 18 seconds. In the interval, they were given an interference task (counting backwards in threes from a three-digit number) to prevent rehearsal.

Findings

Participants were able to recall 90% of the trigrams after 3 seconds, but only 2% after 18 seconds.

Conclusions

This shows that information held in STM has a very short duration before it disappears, if it is not rehearsed. The findings also demonstrate the effects of decay on forgetting.

Criticisms

There was high internal validity — the influence of the independent variable (time) on the dependent variable (recall) was not affected by extraneous variables because the study was conducted in a controlled laboratory situation. There was low external validity because the findings might not apply to other settings (e.g. situations using other kinds of memory).

One study of duration in LTM (Bahrick et al., 1975)

Aims

This studied how long memories remain accessible in a natural context in which it is more likely that one can access very long-term memories (VLTM).

Procedures

400 students of different ages were shown photographs of various people, including photographs from their high school yearbooks, to test face recognition. They were also asked to free-recall names of people they were at high school with.

Findings

The younger participants (who had left high school 15 years before) were 90% accurate in face recall. This dropped to 70% after 48 years. Free recall of names was less good — 60% after 15 years and dropping to 30% after 48 years.

Conclusions

This supports the view that people do have VLTMs which are accurate.

Criticisms

This study had high external (ecological) validity as it was conducted in the real world and tells us more about everyday memory. The study may have had low internal validity because some variables could not be controlled, for example how often an individual still saw ex-classmates or talked about them.

The multi-store model of memory (Atkinson and Shiffrin)

This model proposes that memory is divided into several kinds of store: a sensory store (equivalent to the eyes and ears), a short-term store and a long-term store. Data are passed from one to the other through verbal rehearsal.

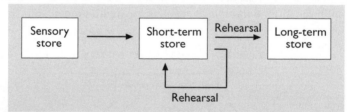

Research evidence

Sperling (1960)

This study demonstrates the existence of the third store — sensory memory. People 'see' more than they remember. What causes this? Five students had to stare at a cross in the centre of a display shown for 50 milliseconds: three rows each with four numbers/letters. After the display a tone was sounded which indicated whether they had to report the top, middle or bottom row, or recall all 12 characters. In the whole report participants typically remembered four or five items (42% recall). In the partial report condition they could recall 75% of the information. This suggests that the data are 'available' in sensory memory for a very brief period but decay quickly so that, if you have to write down all 12 items, they are no longer available.

Glanzer and Cunitz (1966)

Participants were asked to recall word lists; if this was done immediately after being shown the words there was a primacy and a recency effect (early and later words were better recalled) due to STM and LTM effects. If there was a delay of 10 seconds or more there was only a primacy effect. If there was a delay of 10 seconds or more there was only a primacy effect — LTM alone was affected. Primacy is due to the fact that the first items are more likely to have entered LTM. Recency occurs because the last items in the list are still in STM. This demonstrates a difference between STM and LTM.

Evaluation

+ Continues to provide a framework which many psychologists find useful.
+ Can explain research findings on the serial position effect and brain damage (anterograde amnesia involves an inability to store new memories but individuals have intact permanent memory).
− An over-simplification, as both STM and LTM are probably divided into a number of different stores.
− Suggests that memory is a passive process, whereas levels of processing theory and reconstructive memory suggest that it is active.
− The relevance of rehearsal might be an artefact of memory experiments where participants are tested on explicit memory.

The working memory model (Baddeley and Hitch)

Baddeley and Hitch (1974) suggested that short-term memory is more accurately represented in terms of a set of separate stores which handle different modalities (sound and visual data) rather than a single store, as in the multi-store model. The use of the term 'working memory' reflects the idea that this is the area of memory that is active when you are working on information.

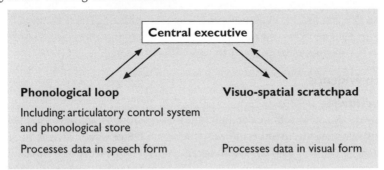

Research evidence

Shallice and Warrington (1970)

This was a case study of KF, who suffered brain damage as a result of a motorcycle accident. KF had no problem with long-term memory, but his digit span was only two items. These findings suggest that different parts of the brain are involved in short-term and long-term memory. It was also found that KF's short-term forgetting of auditory letters and digits was much greater than his forgetting of visual stimuli, and that he could not process verbal materials but could process meaningful sounds. This points to the existence of different stores in short-term (working) memory.

Hitch and Baddeley (1976)

There are two predictions from the working memory model: (1) if two tasks use the same component, they should interfere with each other; (2) if two tasks use different components, their performance should be equally good when conducted together or separately. To test this, participants were given a verbal reasoning task (which should involve the central executive) and a task involving the articulatory loop (saying 'the' repeatedly), or another task using the central executive (saying random digits). As predicted, reasoning performance was slowed down by the additional task only when it involved using the central executive.

> **Evaluation**
>
> + Can explain how we can successfully do two tasks at one time if they involve different stores and why we have trouble with some tasks that involve the same store.
> + Describes rehearsal (the articulatory process) as only one component, which seems more appropriate than the central importance it is given in the multi-store model.
> − The functioning of the central executive is vague and thus can be bent to fit any results.

The levels of processing model (Craik and Lockhart)

Craik and Lockhart (1972) suggested that enduring memories are created through depth of processing rather than a repeated number of analyses (rehearsal). At the shallowest level, processing involves only physical characteristics (such as whether a word is in capital letters or not). The next level is phonemic processing (e.g. considering whether two words rhyme with each other), which leads to an increased memory trace. The deepest level is semantic processing (considering the meaning of a word). 'Depth' can also be achieved through elaboration, organisation and distinctiveness, i.e. depth is determined in terms of the meaning extracted.

Research evidence

Craik and Tulving (1975)

The research aim here was to demonstrate that memory is an automatic by-product of semantic processing. Participants were shown a list of words (five-letter, concrete nouns such as 'table') and for each asked a question with a yes/no answer. The question was one of three types: case (shallow processing, such as 'Is the word in capital letters?'), rhyme (phonemic processing, such as 'Does the word rhyme with "able"?'), sentence (semantic or deep processing, such as 'Would the word fit in the sentence "They met a…in the street"?'). Those words processed semantically were recalled best and those processed phonemically were recalled second best.

Eysenck and Eysenck (1980)

Can distinctiveness enhance memory? Participants were asked to say words in a non-semantic, distinctive condition (e.g. pronouncing the 'b' in 'comb') or a non-semantic, non-distinctive condition (e.g. saying the word 'comb' normally). There were also semantic distinctive and non-distinctive conditions where these words were additionally processed for meaning. Recall was almost as good in the non-semantic, distinctive condition as for the semantic conditions. This shows that distinctiveness can be as powerful as meaning in terms of enhancing memory for words.

Evaluation

+ Can explain anterograde amnesia (processing too shallow to enable retrieval).
+ Recognises variation in ability to recall material because recall is a function of the variety of ways that we deal with data.
– Definition of depth is circular; there is no way to verify how deeply something is processed except in terms of how memorable it is.
– The model ignores the evidence that supports the distinction between STM and LTM.

Forgetting

Specification content

Explanations of forgetting in short-term memory (e.g. decay and displacement). Explanations of forgetting in long-term memory (e.g. retrieval failure and interference). Research into the role of emotional factors in forgetting, including flashbulb memories and repression (e.g. Freud).

Forgetting in short-term memory (STM) can be explained rather differently from forgetting in long-term memory (LTM) because STM is a limited capacity store and therefore information might disappear because of space restrictions. The specification provides *examples* of suitable explanations but you can use any examples you choose as long as you are familiar with more than one explanation for both STM and LTM. You should also be familiar with relevant research evidence to support your explanations, and any potential strengths and/or weaknesses in the studies and/or explanations.

Emotion can enhance (**flashbulb memory**) or reduce (**repression**) recall of events. Your study of repression can, but need not necessarily, refer to Freud's ideas on this topic. Again you are required to explain the concepts (flashbulb memory and repression) and have a critical awareness of appropriate research evidence.

Explanations of forgetting in short-term memory

STM is a limited capacity store and therefore forgetting is likely to be due to loss of availability. One explanation is **decay**, whereby forgetting is due to the spontaneous physical disappearance of the memory trace. However, the disappearance might be due to **displacement** by new material rather than decay; if nothing else entered STM, the memory trace might not disappear. According to the displacement explanation, as STM has limited capacity, when it is full the earlier material will be displaced if it has not been moved to LTM.

Research evidence for decay

Peterson and Peterson (1959)

This study is described on page 13. The procedure involved preventing participants from rehearsing the trigrams displayed. The outcome was that, after 18 seconds, participants could recall very little (only about 10% of the information). This suggests that forgetting in STM is a consequence of the memory trace disappearing (i.e. decaying).

The problem with this explanation is that it is difficult to know whether the lack of recall is actually due to decay or whether there was other information absorbed at the same time, which displaced the original material. The participants in Peterson and Peterson's experiment had to count to prevent rehearsal; the numbers might have displaced the trigrams in STM.

Research evidence for displacement

Waugh and Norman (1965)

Participants were presented with 16 numbers over a period of 1 minute. Then one number was repeated (called the 'probe') and the participant had to recall the number that came immediately afterwards. If the probe number was near the end of the list, recall was high because the number was still in STM. If the probe was early in the list, recall fell dramatically, presumably because the number had been displaced by the subsequent material. The numbers were given at either 1 or 4 second intervals, but in both conditions the rate of forgetting was identical, i.e. the same percentage was forgotten if the probe was the fifth item. This shows that forgetting is not related to time elapsed and therefore demonstrates that forgetting must be due to displacement and not decay.

Explanations of forgetting in long-term memory

LTM has potentially infinite capacity and duration, therefore forgetting is likely to be due to lack of accessibility.

One explanation of forgetting in LTM is **interference** whereby one set of information competes with another, causing it to be 'overwritten' or physically destroyed. There is **proactive interference** (earlier data interfere with new data) and **retroactive interference** (new data interfere with recall of older data). Interference is most likely to occur when two sets of data are similar, which is not a common aspect of real-world memory. **Cue-dependent forgetting (retrieval failure)** describes forgetting as a result of the absence of suitable retrieval cues. Cues might be in terms of associated words, category names, context or mood.

Research evidence for interference

McGeoch and McDonald (1931)

Participants were given lists of adjectives to learn, followed by an interpolated task, and then asked to recall. If the interpolated task was a list of synonyms of the original list, recall was poor (12%), nonsense syllables interfered less (26% recall) while numbers led to 37% recall. Only interference can explain such findings.

LTM: Baddeley and Hitch (1977)

In order to separate out the effects of time (decay) and interference, rugby players were asked to recall the teams they had played during the season. Players varied in the number of games they had played over the same time span, so some would experience more interference when they tried to recall fixtures. The players who had played more games recalled proportionately fewer names, presumably because of interference.

Research evidence for cue-dependent forgetting

Tulving and Psotka (1971)

Participants were given up to six word lists, each with 24 words, organised into six different categories. There was strong evidence of retroactive interference because participants who were only given one or two lists were able to recall a higher percentage of their words than those who had more lists. However, this only occurred in the free recall condition. In a cued recall test, the effects of retroactive interference disappeared. No matter how many lists the participants were given, recall was the same (about 70%) for each list when they were given category names as cues. This means that interference had not caused unlearning, it only *appeared* to have this effect. The memories were available, but not accessible.

Research into the role of emotional factors in forgetting

One study of flashbulb memory (Conway et al., 1994)

Aims

To demonstrate flashbulb memories, one needs an event that has important consequences for people's lives. Conway et al. felt that the resignation of Mrs Thatcher was appropriately consequential and therefore should produce flashbulb memories, if they exist.

Procedures

Participants were interviewed a few days after her resignation and again 11 months later about their flashbulb memories. As a control, interviews were also conducted with people in other countries who would not have experienced flashbulb memories surrounding the event.

Findings

They found that 86% of UK participants still had flashbulb memories 11 months later, whereas only 29% did in other countries. The UK memories were quite detailed and consistent over time.

Conclusions

People do form flashbulb memories of the details surrounding an event of emotional significance. Such memories are more accurate and consistent than memories for events of less emotional significance.

Criticisms

It may not be reasonable to assume that Mrs Thatcher's resignation was emotionally significant for everyone in the UK (though it would be difficult to explain the results differently). It is also possible that the initial interviews meant that memories were rehearsed and thus enhanced.

One study of repression (Myers and Brewin, 1994)

Aims
'Repressors' are characterised by low anxiety and high defensiveness, i.e. they tend to use repression as a coping strategy. Do repressors have restricted access to negative childhood memories?

Procedures
Twenty-seven female undergraduates were classed as repressors or non-repressors. The participants were asked to recall unhappy childhood memories as quickly as possible and were also questioned about their relationships with their parents. This was necessary in order to check that the repressors did have something to repress.

Findings
The repressors took about twice as long to recall unhappy memories. Repressors were also more likely to report poor or negative relationships with their fathers.

Conclusions
This suggests that the slower recall was not a result of having fewer anxiety-provoking memories because these individuals actually had more of such memories. Therefore, they must have been repressing them.

Criticisms
It might be argued that forgetting was due to inhibited recall rather than repression. A further criticism relates to the nature of natural experiments — we are not justified in reaching causal conclusions where the independent variable has not been directly manipulated, or where the participants have not been randomly allocated to groups.

Critical issue: eyewitness testimony

Specification content

Memory research into eyewitness testimony, including reconstructive memory (Bartlett), Loftus's research into this area (e.g. the role of leading questions) and memory for faces (e.g. accuracy of recognition and recall).

Our knowledge of memory, and forgetting, can be applied to a real-world example — **eyewitness testimony**. The main issue concerns the reliability (or unreliability) of recall and this can be considered in terms of **reconstructive memory**. You need to consider research evidence relating to reconstructive memory as well as being able to describe the theory. Elizabeth Loftus has produced a wealth of research in relation to eyewitness testimony and you are specifically required to be familiar with some of her studies, as well as the positive and negative criticisms of them. Finally, eyewitness testimony often relies on **memory for faces**. You are required to have a critical understanding of research evidence relating to face recognition and recall.

Eyewitness testimony (EWT)

EWT is generally accepted as unreliable. The Devlin Committee (1976) recommended that it was not safe to convict on a single EWT alone. Yet juries are quite convinced by it.

EWT is likely to rely on reconstructive memory because memory is a reconstructive process, especially in eyewitnesses who might not have realised that they would need to remember the events. In some cases, the stress of the occasion might have affected their ability to take in all the details. EWT is also affected by leading questions (see Loftus's research).

One study of eyewitness testimony (Loftus and Palmer, 1974)

Aims

This study investigated the accuracy of memory for complex events, such as a traffic accident, and the influence of post-event information on recall.

Procedures

Participants were shown a film clip of a car accident and asked, amongst other things, to estimate the speed the cars were going when they hit each other. In a follow-up, participants returned to the laboratory after a week and were asked to recall aspects of the car accident, most importantly: 'Did you see any broken glass?'.

Findings

If the word 'smashed' was used instead of 'hit', the participants estimated higher speeds. In the follow-up, the group given the word 'smashed' in the original descriptions were twice as likely to answer 'yes' to seeing broken glass (though there was none) than those who had been given the word 'hit'.

Conclusions

This shows that the perception was influenced by the language (leading questions) that was used and that post-event information (the use of the word 'smashed' in later questioning) affects subsequent recall of information.

Criticisms

There is evidence from real-life studies that recall is not affected by post-event information, possibly because the original image is stronger (enhanced by emotional arousal surrounding the event). For example, Christianson and Hubinette (1993) found that witnesses to real bank robberies remembered details accurately. This was more true of those who had been threatened at the time (greater emotional arousal) than those who had not.

Reconstructive memory

Bartlett (1932) suggested that recall is not a matter of passively accessing a piece of information and 'reading it' (as suggested by the multi-store model). It involves active reconstruction based on prior knowledge (schema). Such schema lead to distortions of memory during both storage and recall.

One study of reconstructive memory (Bartlett, 1932)

Aims
This aimed to demonstrate how memory is reconstructed by social schema by studying recall under particular circumstances — when encountering unfamiliar schema. (This should force the individual to adapt the story or picture according to their own schema.)

Procedures
Bartlett gave participants various passages to read or line drawings to reproduce, and asked them to recall them after several days, months or even years (serial reproduction). The passages were deliberately chosen for their unusualness, such as 'War of the Ghosts', because then participants are forced to make distortions based on prior knowledge (schema) in order to remember the story.

Findings
He found that participants tended to make the following changes: rationalisations, omissions, changes of order, alterations in importance, and distortion of emotion. These changes reflected the influence of schema on recall.

Conclusions
People have a drive to make sense of what they encounter and actively construct their memory. This construction is a social act (using cultural schema).

Criticisms
Bartlett's methods were not highly controlled, so experimenter bias may have affected performance. Subsequent research (e.g. Wynn and Logie, 1998) tested recall of real-life events and found more accurate recall. The concept of reconstructive memory cannot explain instances when memory is perfectly accurate, such as learning the lines of a poem.

Other research evidence

Loftus and Zanni (1975)
Leading questions were again tested in this experiment. Participants were shown a short film of a car accident and asked 'Did you see the broken headlight?' or 'Did you see a broken headlight?' The use of 'the' assumes that there was a broken headlight. There was no broken headlight in the film, but 17% of those asked about *the* broken headlight said there was one, whereas only 7% of those asked about *a* broken headlight said they had seen it.

Loftus (1979)
Participants were asked to wait in a room prior to an experiment. While waiting they either heard a man muttering about machine failure, who then walked through the room holding a pen and with grease on his hands, or they heard a hostile exchange of words and breaking glass, followed by a man emerging holding a paper-knife covered in blood. They were given 50 photos and asked to identify the man. They were correct 49% of the time with the man with the pen and 33% of the time with the

man with the knife. This finding has been described as 'weapon focus' and demonstrates the effects of anxiety on recall.

Wells et al. (1979)

This study demonstrated both the lack of accuracy and the believability of EWT. Participants were asked to wait in a cubicle until the experiment started, during which time a confederate appeared and stole a calculator that had been lying there. When the participants were asked to identify the 'thief' from a set of six photographs, only 58% were correct. When the same participants were asked to 'testify' at a mock trial, 80% of them were believed by the jury.

Cohen (1981)

The effects of schema on initial storage and recall were demonstrated in a study in which participants were shown a video of a woman talking with a man, first while eating dinner and then during an informal birthday celebration. The woman was described beforehand as either a waitress or a librarian. When participants were later asked to recall things in the video, they recollected items in line with the stereotypes they had been given. For example, whether or not the woman had books (librarian stereotype) or went bowling (waitress stereotype). This shows that what one remembers is related to stereotypes/schema.

Memory for faces

EWT relies on memory for faces, usually of (1) unfamiliar faces, (2) in poor conditions, (3) and matching real faces against a motionless photograph or Identikit picture.

Bruce and Young (1986) proposed a model for face recognition which suggests that different mechanisms are involved in familiar and unfamiliar face recognition. This is supported by research with brain-damaged patients. Recognition of unfamiliar faces may involve feature detection, whereas familiar face recognition involves configural recognition.

One study of memory for faces (Bruce and Valentine, 1988)

Aims

When considering memory for faces, still photographs are often used to test recognition. However, this ignores the fact that faces are normally in motion. To what extent is motion an important aspect of face recognition?

Procedures

Small lights were attached to all areas of a face and the face was filmed in motion in the dark.

Findings

Participants could identify the facial expressions (e.g. smiling or frowning) and sometimes could identify the person on the basis of the movements alone.

Conclusions

This can explain why people often appear to be quite good at face recognition in psychology experiments but not in real life when having to identify a face from a still photograph. In psychology experiments, neither the face stimulus nor the recognition stimulus is in motion, whereas in real life you have to match a face in motion with a still picture.

Criticisms

This only illustrates one aspect of memory for faces, but it does indicate that there is more to face recognition than feature identification.

Human memory: defining the terms

capacity: a measure of how much material can be contained in STM or LTM. STM is measured in terms of bits or chunks and may hold 7±2 items. LTM is thought to have an infinite capacity for information which may be facts or directions on how to do things.

duration: a measure of how long information is held in memory. STM is defined in terms of the short duration of material in this store. If it is not rehearsed, information disappears or is overwritten. LTM has potentially infinite duration, for example our memory for riding a bicycle.

encoding: the form in which information is stored in memory. Information tends to be stored in an acoustic code (i.e. the sound of a word) in STM and to be stored semantically (i.e. according to meaning) in LTM.

eyewitness testimony (EWT): the descriptions given in a criminal trial by individuals who were present around the time of the crime. Such descriptions may include an identification of the criminals, important details of the sequence of events, who or what else was present and/or peripheral information, such as the weather that day.

flashbulb memory: an accurate and long-lasting memory formed at a time of intense emotion, such as a significant public or personal event. It is details of the context in which the memory was created that is the flashbulb memory rather than the event itself. It is as if a flash photograph was taken at the moment of the event and every detail indelibly printed in memory.

forgetting: the inability to recall or recognise information that was previously learned or placed in memory. The act of forgetting assumes that something was once stored in memory and now has disappeared (is not available), or cannot be brought to mind (is not accessible).

levels of processing model of memory: the suggestion that memories become enduring because of the way they are processed. Information that is deeply processed is better remembered. Depth can be achieved through meaning, elaboration, organisation and distinctiveness.

long-term memory (LTM): relatively permanent storage which has unlimited capacity and duration. Four different kinds of LTM have been identified: procedural memory (knowing how), declarative memory (knowing that), semantic memory (facts) and episodic memory (events). There is also a distinction made between explicit and implicit memory: remembrance because you were instructed to do so or recall without conscious storage of data.

memory: the process by which we retain information. It includes the encoding, storage and retrieval of experience, i.e. placing information in memory in some physical form, creating an enduring trace of some experiences and being able to re-locate these experiences for use at a later time.

memory for faces: the ability to recognise and recall faces. This can involve the recall of familiar or unfamiliar faces, which may involve different processes. Feature-by-feature recognition may not explain how we recall faces, but the overall organisation of the features may be more important.

multi-store model of memory: an account of how information becomes stored in our minds in terms of a multiple number of stores which are different in terms of capacity, duration and encoding. Information enters our minds in the form of sensory perceptions (a sensory store) which, if attended to, are passed to a short-term store where they are held for a brief period unless rehearsed. Rehearsal ultimately leads to transfer to long-term store.

reconstructive memory: an explanation of how we store and recollect long-term memories in terms of social and cultural processes. Initial comprehension is affected by stereotypes and schema, so that memories are distorted predictably. Subsequent recall is a process of reconstruction of fragments, again biased by cultural stereotypes and schema.

repression: A method of keeping anxiety-provoking material out of conscious aware-ness as a means of coping (also called 'motivated forgetting'). Freud proposed that it is a form of ego-defense and that such repressed material surfaces elsewhere, such as in dreams or Freudian slips.

short-term memory (STM): a temporary place for storing data where it receives minimal processing. This store is limited in capacity (7±2 items) and duration (probably less than 18 seconds). Information tends to be stored acoustically (how it sounds) rather than semantically (in terms of meaning).

working memory model: a more detailed account of STM which suggests that one area of memory is dedicated to dealing with the information we are currently working on. This information is handled by a phonological loop (acoustic data) and/or a visuo-spatial scratchpad (visual data). The management of these stores is organised by a central executive.

Developmental psychology: attachments in development

The development and variety of attachments

Specification content

The development of attachments (e.g. Schaffer). Research into individual differences, including secure and insecure attachments (e.g. Ainsworth) and cross-cultural variations. Explanations of attachment (e.g. learning theory, Bowlby's theory).

Infants become attached to their caregivers and this process follows a sequence of different stages. Schaffer has offered one account of this sequence but you can equally use others.

It is important to recognise that the development of attachments varies between individuals (individual differences), for example some infants are **securely attached** whereas others are **insecurely attached**. You are required to study these differences as they are included in the specification. The distinction between secure and insecure attachments stems from Ainsworth's research using the **Strange Situation**. In addition to individual differences there are cultural differences or variations in how children are attached to caregivers.

Explanations of attachments offer an account of how and why children become attached to a caregiver. The best-known and most developed explanation is Bowlby's theory, but there are others such as learning theory and also Freud's theory. The specification requires that you are familiar with at least two explanations.

The development of attachments

Schaffer (1996) outlined the following phases based on his own (Schaffer and Emerson, 1964) and Bowlby's (1969) research:

- *Phase 1: pre-attachment — indiscriminate social responsiveness (birth to 2 months).* Infants are friendly towards other people and show very limited ability to discriminate between them. They are equally friendly to inanimate objects. Towards the end of this period they are more content when with people.
- *Phase 2: attachment in the making — recognition of familiar people (2 to 6/7 months).* Infants continue to be generally social, but there is beginning to be a marked difference of behaviour towards one mother-figure or primary caregiver. Infants continue to be relatively easily comforted by anyone.

- *Phase 3: clear-cut attachments — separation protest and stranger anxiety (around 7 months).* The infant shows attachment to a primary caregiver through separation protest (protesting when left and joy at reunion) and stranger anxiety. Shortly after the main attachment is formed, the infant also develops a wider circle of attachments, depending on how many consistent relationships he/she has (multiple attachments). All attachments are important but the primary attachment remains qualitatively different from all other relationships. Separation protest and stranger anxiety disappear after the age of 2.
- *Phase 4: goal-corrected partnership — two-sided relationships (2 years, approximately).* The child develops insight into the mother-figure's behaviour. This enables a reciprocal relationship to develop, and is the basis of adult relationships.

Research into individual differences

One study of secure and insecure attachment (Ainsworth and Bell, 1971)

Aims

In order to investigate attachment behaviour, a method of assessment was needed and so the Strange Situation, a method of controlled observation, was devised.

Procedures

The Strange Situation procedure consists of seven 3-minute episodes where the infant is left by the caregiver with a stranger, reunited with the caregiver, and left entirely alone — in various combinations. The key behaviours that are used to assess attachment are:

- separation anxiety — a securely attached child shows some anxiety but is fairly easily soothed
- infants' willingness to explore — a more securely attached child will explore more widely
- stranger anxiety — security of attachment is related to greater stranger anxiety
- reunion behaviour — insecurely attached children might ignore the caregiver's return

Findings

Ainsworth and Bell found that 71% of infants were securely attached. They showed some distress on separation but were relatively easily consoled, and greeted their caregiver enthusiastically on return. Their caregivers were sensitive in responding. The other infants were classed as insecurely attached, either avoidant (12%) or resistant (17%). The avoidant infants were indifferent when the caregiver left and did not display stranger anxiety. At reunion, they actively avoided contact with caregiver, and the caregiver generally ignored the infant during play. The resistant infants were seriously distressed when their caregiver left and not easily consoled when the caregiver returned. The caregiver showed inconsistent behaviour.

Conclusions

There is evidence for different types of attachment; certain sets of behaviours regularly occurred together. The 'norm' would appear to be secure attachment.

Criticisms

Infants who are more used to separation might show less distress, which would decrease the validity of this form of assessment, as you are assessing individuals' experiences rather than their attachments. There may be other attachment types, for example Main and Solomon (1986) identified another kind of attachment — insecure/disorganised — where an infant shows no set patterns of behaviour at separation or reunion.

One study of cross-cultural variation (Van Ijzendoorn and Kroonenberg, 1988)

Aims

This Dutch study sought to compare attachment rates (as measured by the Strange Situation) in different countries, in order to consider cross-cultural variations.

Procedures

Over 2000 Strange Situation classifications from 32 studies conducted in 8 different countries were examined by using a meta-analysis — an analysis that involves grouping together the findings from a number of different studies. The studies were selected by searching through psychology journals to find any that had used the Strange Situation to measure attachment.

Findings

Some of the findings are shown in the following table:

Country	Number of studies	Percentage of each attachment type (to the nearest whole number)		
		Secure	Avoidant	Resistant
West Germany	3	57	35	8
Great Britain	1	75	22	3
Netherlands	4	67	26	7
Japan	2	68	5	27
China	1	50	25	25
USA	18	65	21	14

Conclusions

The findings indicate that secure attachment is the norm in all countries, but that there are important variations. It is possible that such similarity is due to increasing exposure to a common media (TV and books). Cross-cultural differences may be due to different parenting styles.

Criticisms

One should take into account the generally small samples and, most importantly, the fact that the Strange Situation may not be a valid form of assessment in other cultures. For example, in Japan infants rarely leave their mother, so they are more likely to exhibit distress in the Strange Situation — not because of insecure attachment but because they have little experience of separation.

Learning theory

Dollard and Miller (1950) argued that the hungry infant feels uncomfortable, which creates a drive to lessen the discomfort. When the infant is fed, this reduces the discomfort and the drive. Drive reduction is rewarding and the infant learns that food is a reward or primary reinforcer. The person who supplies the food is associated with pleasure/reward and becomes a secondary (or conditioned) reinforcer, and a source of reward in his/her own right.

Research evidence

Harlow (1959)

Harlow aimed to test the hypothesis that feeding was the basis of attachment. He provided young monkeys with two wire 'mothers', one with a feeding bottle attached and the other covered in cloth (contact comfort). The infants spent most time with the cloth mother. This demonstrated that, in monkeys at least, attachment was not related to feeding. A further finding from this study was that contact comfort alone was insufficient for healthy emotional development as these monkeys later had difficulty in reproductive relationships. This shows that interaction is also important.

One must be careful about generalising this to human behaviour. In addition, there was a confounding variable in this study, in so far as the two wire 'mothers' had different shaped heads. One of the 'heads' might have been more appealing.

Schaffer and Emerson (1964)

This study followed 60 Scottish babies for 18 months, observing them in their own homes every 4 weeks and assessing attachment in terms of separation and stranger anxiety. They found that the first specific attachments appeared between 6 and 9 months. Soon after this, other attachments formed and by 18 months very few (13%) were attached to only one person. In 39% of the cases the person who usually fed, bathed and changed the child was *not* the child's primary attachment object. There were individual differences in terms of infant temperament (e.g. some infants preferred to be cuddled whereas others didn't) and maternal responsiveness (infants were most attached to mothers who showed higher responsiveness). This suggests that attachment can be best understood in terms of the various relationships that an infant forms with those who stimulate and respond to him/her.

Bowlby's theory

According to Bowlby:
- attachment is adaptive. Attachment behaviour promotes survival because it ensures safety and food for offspring.
- attachments develop between an infant and a caregiver because the infant elicits care via social releasers (characteristics such as looking cute or crying) and some adults respond sensitively to these cues. Attachment is a mutual bond.

- attachment is a biological (innate) process and there is a critical period for its development. Beyond the age of 2½ years is too late.
- the attachment relationship serves as a template for future relationships. The infant develops internal working models (schema) to represent experience. One of these models concerns relationships and is based on the relationship with one's primary caregiver. Bowlby's concept of monotropy was that one relationship is qualitatively different from all others and this is the one on which the internal working model is based.

Research evidence

Hazan and Shaver (1987)

Are styles of adult romantic relationships related to early attachment experiences? A 'Love Quiz' was printed in a newspaper to assess: (1) early attachment experiences; (2) later experiences of adult romantic love; and (3) beliefs about romantic love. Hazan and Shaver found that respondents who were securely attached as infants had trusting and lasting love relationships. Anxious, ambivalent types worried that their partners didn't really love them. Avoidant lovers typically feared intimacy, and believed that they did not need love to be happy. This supports the view that early attachments act as a template for the future.

However, one should remember that the data are correlational, and therefore we cannot be certain that early attachment caused later romantic style. The findings are also dependent on retrospective recall.

Tronick et al. (1992)

This study recorded observations of an African cultural group in Zaire, the Efe, who live in extended family groups. The infants were looked after and even breast-fed by different women, but usually they slept with their own mother at night. Despite contact with many different caregivers the infants still, by the age of 6 months, did show one primary attachment. This supports Bowlby's concept of monotropy.

Evaluation

+ Bowlby's theory has had an enormous impact, for example in terms of hospital care of children (where bond disruption is now avoided).
- The notion that attachment is adaptive is unfalsifiable (can't be proven wrong), though it is plausible.
- The concept of a critical period might be too strong. There could be a sensitive period. Evidence related to privation supports the view that children who fail to become attached do suffer permanent emotional consequences.
- The internal working model would lead us to expect children to form similar sorts of relationships with all people, because the individual is always working from the same template. However, the correlations among a child's various relationships are actually quite low (Howes et al., 1994).

Deprivation and privation

Specification content

Research into both the short- and long-term effects of deprivation/separation (including Bowlby's maternal deprivation hypothesis) and privation (e.g. Hodges and Tizard's study of institutionalisation).

Bowlby's **maternal deprivation hypothesis** is given as an 'including' and therefore you must be able to describe this hypothesis. Deprivation refers to the *loss* of attachments through **separation** and **deprivation**, and **privation** refers to the *lack* of attachments (i.e. no attachments were ever formed). Hodges and Tizard's research is given as an example of a suitable study of the long-term effects of privation.

Deprivation and separation

Note that a child can be separated from a primary caregiver but experience no deprivation *if there is no bond disruption*. Separation does not necessarily mean deprivation. **Bond disruption** refers to no continuity of emotional care.

Short-term effects: the protest–despair–detachment (PDD) model

Robertson and Bowlby (1952) observed young children who were separated from their mothers and identified the following:

(1) **Protest** — the children's initial response was to be very distressed but they could be comforted. They were inwardly angry and fearful.
(2) **Despair** — eventually the children became calmer, though apathetic. They might seek self-comfort through, for example, thumb-sucking or rocking.
(3) **Detachment** — if the situation continued for weeks or months, the child might have appeared to be coping but was unresponsive. The return of the caregiver might be ignored.

One study of the short-term effects of deprivation (Robertson and Robertson, 1968)

Aims

A series of films was made to show the distress experienced by children during brief separations from primary caregivers, and also to show the positive effects of substitute emotional care.

Procedures

Data were collected at regular intervals using a film camera. It was important to sample behaviour regularly, in order to prevent any bias (e.g. just filming when the child was crying). The films included Laura who spent 8 days in hospital, John who was in a residential nursery for 9 days and four other children who spent time in foster care (with the Robertsons).

Findings

The children without substitute emotional care (John and Laura) were very distressed and became detached during their time in hospital. They were very resistant when reunited with their parents. The children cared for in the foster home appeared content and welcomed their parents when reunited.

Conclusions

Substitute emotional care can prevent emotional deprivation during periods of brief separation. This shows that separation does not necessarily lead to deprivation.

Criticisms

Barrett (1997) argued that there are individual differences. Secure children cope relatively well with separation, whereas insecure children have more difficulties.

Long-term effects: the maternal deprivation hypothesis

Prior to formulating the attachment theory, Bowlby (1951) proposed that children who experienced maternal deprivation would experience permanent emotional damage. He outlined the then radical idea that emotional deprivation might be as serious for psychological adjustment as the lack of vitamins are for physical health. Until this hypothesis was formulated it was thought that such children simply required a good standard of physical care, for example if they were hospitalised.

One study of the long-term effects of deprivation (Bowlby, 1946)

Aims

The aim of this study was to test the maternal deprivation hypothesis.

Procedures

Case histories of 44 patients were examined. They were distinguished by the fact that they were 'thieves' — children who were referred to the clinic because they had committed certain crimes. Bowlby compared these children with 44 other maladjusted children.

Findings

A large number of the 'thieves' were diagnosed as 'affectionless', i.e. having little emotional responsiveness; 86% of these affectionless children had, before the age of 2, experienced repeated separations from their primary caregiver. Bowlby termed this disaffected state affectionless psychopathy

Conclusions

Affectionless psychopathy is caused by attachment bonds being disturbed before the critical age of $2\frac{1}{2}$.

Criticisms

Some of the important data were collected retrospectively and might have been unreliable. In addition, some children had in fact been separated from their mothers for very short periods. It is hard to see why separation would have had such a major impact in these cases.

Privation

Privation refers to the experience of never having formed attachments, as distinct from deprivation, where a child has previously experienced attachment.

One study of the long-term effects of privation (Hodges and Tizard, 1989)

Aims

This tested the maternal deprivation hypothesis by looking at the effects of institutional care on subsequent development. The children in the study could be said to have experienced emotional privation because they were placed in the institution before the age of 4 months (before attachments form) and had an average of 50 different caretakers in their first 4 years who were instructed not to form attachments.

Procedures

This was a longitudinal study (the children were followed up at 4, 8 and 16 years) and a natural experiment (some of the children remained in the institution, some were adopted and some returned to their natural homes). It involved 65 children at the outset.

Findings

Follow-up studies at age 4 and 8 found that the adopted children did best in virtually every way when compared with those who returned home ('restored' children). A further follow-up study at age 16 assessed some of the children. The adopted children had good family relationships, whereas the 'restored' children were less likely to be closely attached. Both groups of children (adopted and restored) had problems with relationships outside the home, for example they were less likely to have a special friend, and were more quarrelsome than other children.

Conclusions

The findings at age 4 and 8 run counter to Bowlby's belief that a child's natural home is best, and also that recovery is not possible. The later findings suggest that early privation may have had effects on relationships after all. The children could conduct good relationships with others as long as the others were supportive.

Criticisms

One problem with this study is that the most 'attractive' children were chosen to be adopted. There was also participant 'drop-out' which biased the final sample. Those adopted children who were left in the study were the ones who, at age 4, had *fewer* adjustment problems, whereas the remaining 'restored' children had initially had the most adjustment problems.

Other research evidence

Rutter et al. (1998)

Recent access to children from Romania has permitted further assessment of the effects of privation. This study followed just over one hundred Romanian orphans adopted in the UK before the age of 2. When the orphans first arrived in the UK they were physically and mentally underdeveloped, but by the age of 4 all had improved, presumably as a result of the better care they were receiving. Those children who were adopted latest showed the slowest improvements, which appears to support the view that the poorer the early experience the more there is to recover from. However, the evidence does show that recovery is possible given good subsequent care.

Case studies

A number of case studies have been cited as evidence for the effects of privation. Genie (Curtiss, 1989) spent her early life locked in a room. She received help at the age of $13\frac{1}{2}$ years but never properly recovered, emotionally or cognitively. This could be because she was retarded from birth or because she never received consistent emotional care after her 'discovery'. It is worth noting that her mother claimed to have been attached to Genie through her imprisonment at the hands of her father.

The Czechoslovakian twins PM and JM (Koluchová, 1976) were locked in a cupboard for much of their first 7 years. They were then looked after by two loving sisters and by age 14 had near normal intellectual and social functioning. They did have each other during their isolation, were 'discovered' at an earlier age, and went to a loving home.

Conclusions from these and other studies suggest that age can matter (a sensitive period). We cannot know what attachment experiences these children had, both before and after their isolation, nor how they might have developed even if they had not been isolated. Furthermore, it is difficult to separate emotional from physical deprivation; later maladjustment might be due to physical deprivation.

Evaluation

+ Children who suffer early privation are also likely to continue to experience disruption, and later maladjustment might be due to this, rather than early privation. When children have better experiences later, they can cope well.
+ There are individual differences. Some children appear to be unable to recover, as in the case of reactive attachment disorder, where a child appears permanently unable to form relationships. Such children often have a history of late adoption (after the age of 6 months), followed by multiple foster homes. They do not recover and continue to show little emotion and no conscience.

Critical issue: day-care

Specification content

The effects of day-care on children's cognitive and social development.

Research on attachment led some people to believe that when a child is placed in **day-care** the consequent separation from his/her primary caregiver would have detrimental effects on the child's development. Separation might affect cognitive and/or **social development**.

Negative effects of day-care on children's cognitive development

It is possible that day-care negatively affects cognitive development.

Research evidence

Howes (1990)

This study followed a group of children who had been in day-care before they were 1 year old. In their first year of school, teachers rated them as being very easily distracted and less considerate than others. However, these children had been in poor-quality day-care.

Tizard (1979)

Conversations between a mother and her child were rated as more complex than those between a child and a nursery-school teacher. Mothers had more exchanges and elicited more from the children. This is likely to be due to the fact that teachers have to divide their attention between a number of children, but they also inevitably know the children less well and have less of a personal sense of investment in the child. This suggests that day-care might have a negative effect on cognitive development.

Positive effects of day-care on children's cognitive development

Some research suggests that day-care has a positive effect on cognitive development.

Research evidence

Kagan et al. (1980)

The researchers set up their own nursery in Boston where each member of staff had responsibility for a small group of children, thus ensuring close emotional contact. The 33 infants were studied over 2-years and compared with 67 control infants cared for by their mothers at home. Kagan et al. found no consistently large differences between the two groups of children on social, emotional or cognitive variables. There was large variability among all the children, but it was not related to the form of care.

Heber et al. (1972)

Operation Headstart was a day-care programme in the USA designed to offer disadvantaged children extra stimulation so that, when they started school, they were no longer at a disadvantage. The programme was not as successful as was hoped. Heber et al. suggested that perhaps the day-care had not started early enough. In the Milwaukee project Heber et al. worked with newborn infants and their low social class Black mothers who had IQs below 75. Half the group were 'controls' and received no extra treatment. The mothers in the experimental group were given help with job-related skills, parenting and housekeeping, and their children were involved in a regular day-care programme from the age of 3 months. By the time the children entered school, the experimental group had a mean IQ of 124 whereas the control group's IQ was 94. By the age of 10 there was still a 10-point IQ difference.

Negative effects of day-care on children's social development

An alternative approach is to consider the effects of day-care on social development.

Research evidence

Belsky and Rovine (1988)

This study assessed attachment (using the Strange Situation) in infants who had been receiving 20 hours or more of day-care per week before they were 1 year old. These children were found to be more likely to be insecurely attached than a control group of children at home. One should note, however, that many of these children in day-care were securely attached but *more* were insecurely attached than those at home.

The result has been criticised because attachment was assessed using the Strange Situation and day-care children are more accustomed to separation than those at home, and therefore might appear to be insecurely attached.

The National Institute of Child Health and Human Development (1997)

This study examined over 1000 infants (and their mothers) at age 6 months and again at 15 months. The mothers were interviewed and the infants were observed at home or in day-care. The study found no differences between the two groups of children in terms of emotional adjustment, but it did find effects if maternal sensitivity and responsiveness were taken into account. Those infants whose mothers were low in sensitivity/responsiveness were less secure if they were experiencing poor day-care arrangements. The two factors — maternal sensitivity and poor-quality care — did therefore appear to affect development. Maternal sensitivity or poor quality care alone is not sufficient to cause harm.

Positive effects of day-care on children's social development

Some research presents a different and more positive picture for the effects of day-care.

Research evidence

Andersson (1992)

The children in this Swedish study were first assessed at age 4 and a record made of early day-care. They were reassessed at age 8 and 13, using IQ data and teachers' reports. School performance was rated highest in those children who entered day-care before the age of 1 year. School performance was lowest for those who did not have any day-care.

One should note that this study was conducted in Sweden where day-care is high-quality (funded by the government). In addition, those children who did enter day-care before the age of 1 also came from families with higher socio-economic status, which might explain why these children had progressed faster.

Evaluation

+ The research indicates that it is the *quality* of day-care that is most significant. If it is high-quality, and the staff ratios are low, children appear to benefit from day-care.
+ Children who are insecurely attached might benefit. Egeland and Hiester (1995) found that day-care appeared to have a negative effect for secure children but had a positive influence on the insecure children. This may be because other individual differences are also significant. For example, Pennebaker et al. (1981) found that the nursery experience was threatening for those children who were shy and unsociable.

Attachments in development: defining the terms

attachment: a strong emotional and reciprocal tie that develops over time between an infant and its primary caregiver(s) and results in a desire to maintain proximity. Bowlby's theory of attachment suggested that attachment serves an adaptive function: in the short term it ensures safety and closeness, and in the long term it is the basis of emotional development and adult relationships.

day-care: an environment where a child is cared for outside his or her own home by a person other than a relative. This could include childminding, day nurseries and nursery schools.

deprivation: the state of having lost or been dispossessed of something. In relation to attachment it refers to the experience of bond disruption as a consequence of separation from an attachment figure for a period of time (either repeated short-term separations or long-term separation). If there is no bond disruption, then it is 'separation' rather than 'deprivation' that has occurred.

insecure attachment: a form of attachment between an infant and caregiver which is not optimal for healthy development. It may be associated with poor cognitive and/or emotional development. Examples are avoidant, resistant and disorganised attachment. Avoidant attachment is shown, in the Strange Situation, by apparent indifference when the caregiver leaves, and little stranger anxiety. At reunion, the infant actively avoids contact with the caregiver. Resistant attachment is shown by extreme distress when the caregiver goes and resistance to being consoled on his/her return.

maternal deprivation hypothesis: the view that separation from a primary caregiver (maternal deprivation) leads to the breaking of attachment bonds and long-term effects on emotional development. Bowlby (1953) likened maternal deprivation to physical deprivation, suggesting that maternal care was as necessary for healthy development as vitamins were. Note that the term 'maternal' refers to 'mothering' not 'women'. Mothering can be done by anyone.

privation: the lack of any attachments, as distinct from the loss of attachments (deprivation). Privation may lead to permanent emotional damage, whereas deprivation may have less serious consequences.

secure attachment: a strong and contented attachment of an infant to its caregiver, related to healthy cognitive and emotional development. The securely attached infant is able to function independently because its caregiver acts as a secure base. In the Strange Situation, the infant shows a moderate level of seeking closeness to the caregiver. The infant is upset by the caregiver's departure but greets him/her positively on reunion and is readily soothed.

separation: the physical loss of a mother-figure but not necessarily of maternal care, as other people may continue to provide mothering. Separation need not have negative consequences on a child's development.

Questions & Answers

In this section of the guide there are eight questions — four on Cognitive Psychology and four on Developmental Psychology. Each question is worth 30 marks. You should allow 30 minutes when attempting to answer a question, dividing that time according to mark allocation for each part.

The section is structured as follows:
- sample questions in the style of the unit
- example candidate responses at the B/C/D-grade level (candidate A) — these will demonstrate both strengths and weaknesses of responses with potential for improvement
- example candidate responses at the A-grade level (candidate B) — such answers demonstrate thorough knowledge, a good understanding and an ability to deal with the data that are presented in the questions

Examiner's comments

All candidate responses are followed by examiner's comments. These are preceded by the icon ℮. They indicate where credit is due. In the weaker answers, they also point out areas for improvement, specific problems and common errors such as poor time management, lack of clarity, weak or non-existent development, irrelevance, misinterpretation of the question and mistaken meanings of terms.

The comments also indicate how each example answer would have been marked in an actual exam, using the allocations listed on pages 6–7.

Cognitive psychology (I)

(a) **Outline two explanations of forgetting in short-term memory.**   (3 + 3 marks)
(b) **Describe the multi-store model of memory.**   (6 marks)
(c) **'We can learn a lot about the psychological processes involved in long-term
memory by looking at explanations of forgetting.'
To what extent does psychological research into forgetting provide insights
into long-term human memory?**   (18 marks)

Total: 30 marks

(a) You need to select two explanations for forgetting in short-term memory, which might well be decay and displacement as they are named in the specification, but you may select any two. In order to gain full marks you need to demonstrate your understanding of the explanations as if you were communicating with someone who has no knowledge of these concepts. Two or three sentences is about right, though detail and clarity are more important than length.

(b) You need to provide a detailed and accurate explanation of the multi-store model. The detail required is indicated by the marks for the question. You are not expected to provide more than 5–6 minutes' worth of writing, so be selective about what you include (if you feel you know more than this). You are not required to give evidence that supports the model, or to identify weaknesses, but simply to describe what this model suggests about the nature and structure of memory.

(c) In the final part of the question you are always required to provide mainly evaluative commentary. You must take care to avoid being overly descriptive. It may help to outline an argument first and then fill in the details of this argument. So, for example, this question requires you to use research on forgetting to illuminate what we know about memory. You could offer brief details of such research, relating mainly to findings, and use the conclusions to make statements about what this research shows about memory. Alternatively, you might make a general statement about forgetting research (e.g. 'It shows that memories don't disappear, they just can't always be accessed') and then cite studies to support the argument. If you identify several arguments, each supported by one or two studies, this would be a good answer. However, don't overlook AO2, for which you could gain more marks through methodological assessments of the studies.

■ ■ ■

Answer to question 1: candidate A

(a) Forgetting might happen in STM because of spontaneous decay, in other words, if it isn't used it disappears. Forgetting might also happen in STM because of interference.

question

ℓ Both explanations are appropriate. The first one (decay) is provided in more detail than the second one, but it could not be described as detailed. The description offered for interference is basic. (3 out of 6 marks — 2 marks for the first description and 1 mark for the second one.)

(b) The multi-store model of memory states that memory consists of different stores. The stores are sensory memory, short-term memory and long-term memory. Information is passed from one store to another by rehearsal. This can be shown in a diagram.

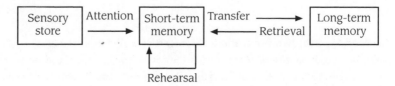

ℓ It is true that a picture is worth a thousand words (almost) but it probably needs a little bit more support than given here in order to demonstrate the candidate's understanding. (3 out of 6 marks — a limited description, generally accurate but closer to lacking detail than detailed.)

(c) Long-term forgetting can mainly be explained in terms of a lack of accessibility. The memory is often there but you can't bring it to mind. This is called the 'tip-of-the-tongue phenomenon'.

An example of lack of accessibility is research that has looked at context-dependent forgetting. If you are tested in the same room where learning took place, then memory is better. This suggests that it is the context which helps make some memories more accessible.

Some research studies give people lists of things to remember and if the participants are then asked to recall the words, they don't do as well as when they are given cues to help them remember, like being given the names of certain categories. This shows that the memories were there; it was just that they couldn't bring them to mind.

Interference is another explanation that is offered for forgetting in long-term memory. The idea is that if you remember one set of data and then later have to learn something else, this will interfere with what you learned first, especially if the material is similar. However, one study found that if you gave people cues to help them remember the first material, then their memories recovered.

All of this is focused on one particular kind of memory — memory for facts. The same things might not be true for the kind of memory where you have to remember how to get home or how to ride a bicycle.

ℓ Candidate A has provided a reasonable response to the question. It is a shame that the evidence that is referred to is rather vague. It is bordering on being detailed but lacks sufficient precision (names and dates would help this). A further problem lies in the depth of analysis. This is generally rather superficial, leaving the examiner to draw his/her own conclusions. For example, 'This shows that the memories were there; it was just that they couldn't bring them to mind' could be explained further in order to make the point clear. Examples of commentary/analysis that have been included occur in paragraph 2, where the candidate has offered commentary in the sentence beginning 'This suggests that...', and again in paragraph 3, 'This shows that...'. In the last paragraph there is some attempt at an analysis. The description of various studies and explanations attracts AO1 credit. As this material is reasonable but less detailed than desirable it receives 4 out of 6 marks. The evaluation is basic but reasonably effective, for a mark of 5 out of 12, giving a total of 9 out of 18 marks.

Total for this question: 15 out of 30 marks

■ ■ ■

Answer to question 1: candidate B

(a) According to displacement theory, old information in STM is pushed out by new information because STM is a limited capacity store. New information displaces what was originally there. The other possibility is that information simply decays in STM if it isn't rehearsed. This is called decay theory and is supported by research that shows that memories decay even when you are asleep, where interference couldn't explain forgetting.

   𝑒 Both descriptions are accurate and detailed, making them worth the maximum marks. (6 out of 6 marks)

(b) The multi-store model of memory explains memory in terms of the existence of several stores: sensory memory is where data enter the processing system. It is equivalent to our senses, i.e. the eyes and ears. Data are held here for a very brief time and will disappear unless they are given attention and passed to the short-term memory store. It is claimed that this is a limited capacity store where it is likely that only about seven chunks of data can be held at any one time. It is chunks rather than items because research has shown that we can hold the same number of items even if some items consist of more 'bits'. Verbal rehearsal maintains data in STM, otherwise it decays or is overwritten by new data. Finally, rehearsal might lead to the data being passed to long-term memory which is distinguished by having infinite capacity and potentially infinite duration.

   𝑒 This is a sound description of the multi-store model, and is detailed and accurate. Long-term memory is perhaps given rather brief coverage but there is sufficient here for full marks. (6 out of 6 marks)

(c) Forgetting can tell us a lot about long-term memory because forgetting is the other side of the coin to remembering. There are various explanations for forgetting in long-term memory. First, there is decay. This suggests that some long-term memories decay over time. However, several studies by Bahrick show that people can remember some things for a very long time (called very long-term memories). For example, they can recognise the faces of classmates 40 years later and, in another study, participants forgot Spanish words they had learned over the first 3 or 4 years after leaving school, but then this forgetting tailed off. Decay is unlikely to be an explanation for forgetting in long-term memory.

Another possible explanation is interference. A study by McGeoch and McDonald (1931) found that forgetting increased when participants had to learn interpolated lists of material, and that forgetting was especially high if the interpolated lists contained similar material. This suggests that long-term memory is affected by subsequent learning except that, in one experiment, Tulving found that if you gave participants cues to help them recall the material, then the effects of interference disappeared.

The importance of this research is that it shows that material is often available but is simply not accessible. This was further demonstrated in an experiment by Tulving when he found that every time participants were asked to recall a list of words, they recalled some different words.

The trouble with much of this research is that it focuses on a particular kind of memory — explicit memory (when you have been told to memorise something) and also on a kind of memory called semantic memory which is not representative of all kinds of long-term memory. Memory for things like riding a bicycle or swimming are not affected in the same way, though learning one skill can interfere with learning a previous skill. An example of this is learning squash after learning tennis because they both involve rather different arm movements and the one skill interferes with the other.

This answer focuses well on the question set, using research evidence (studies and explanations) to consider what we know about memory. Description is kept to a reasonable minimum and is largely introduced with phrases such as 'However, ...' and 'This suggests that ...', which makes effective use of material — an AO2 criterion. Other forms of evaluation are also introduced, such as looking at the types of memory studied and thus the validity of the research. It is desirable to keep description to a minimum because of the greater number of marks for AO2. However, it should not be reduced too much. Slightly more detail would be required here for the full 6 AO1 marks — the range here is limited, for 4 marks out of 6. The AO2 commentary is reasonable and effective, though slightly limited, for 10 out of 12 marks. This makes a total of 14 out of 18 marks.

Total for this question: 26 out of 30 marks

Cognitive psychology (II)

(a) Outline *three* differences between short-term memory and long-term memory. (2+2+2 marks)

(b) Outline findings of research into flashbulb memory. (6 marks)

(c) 'Research into eyewitness testimony suggests that memory is unreliable, yet there are occasions when memory can be quite accurate.'
To what extent does research support the usefulness of eyewitness testimony? (18 marks)

Total: 30 marks

(a) Each difference only attracts 2 marks, so keep your answers simple but ensure that you provide enough detail to show that you understand each difference. You would obtain 1 mark for identifying a difference and indicating some grasp of this difference. For 2 marks you must provide some clear but brief elaboration. You only have about 5 minutes for the whole answer, and this includes thinking time.

(b) In this part you must focus on findings only. 'Research' can include theories as well as studies, so you might report the 'findings' of a theory. The more findings you can cover, the more marks you will attract. This could be in terms of multiple findings from one study and/or various findings from different studies. Two findings would be sufficient for full marks if given in enough detail.

(c) The last part of the question requires analysis and commentary in addition to description. In order to do this, you should focus on the question you are asked, in essence, 'How useful is eyewitness testimony'? Clearly you must refer to relevant research studies but keep the description (AO1) to a minimum because there are more AO2 marks. Use the studies to support points you wish to make, as 'effective use of material' is an AO2 criterion. Aim to provide useful details of the studies, such as the findings. It would be appropriate to mention any strengths or limitations of such studies (e.g. they were conducted in a laboratory) because that is relevant to the validity of the findings, and thus the extent to which the study can inform us about the usefulness of eyewitness testimony.

◼ ◼ ◼

Answer to question 2: candidate A

(a) STM is different from LTM in terms of capacity, duration and encoding. It has less capacity because it can only hold 7 ± 2 items whereas LTM has a potentially infinite capacity. Memories in STM are short, lasting less than 30 seconds, whereas again LTM memories might last for ever. Finally, encoding is different — memories in STM tend to be more acoustic whereas LTM is semantic.

This is a clear and detailed answer, with all differences elaborated in an appropriate manner. 2 marks for each difference. (6 out of 6 marks)

(b) Research studies of flashbulb memory have found that people remember certain events as if they were photographs. For example, one study asked people to recall what they were doing when Mrs Thatcher resigned and people in this country could remember more about what they were doing than people in other countries. This is because the event had more emotional significance for them and therefore it created a flashbulb memory. Another finding is from an experiment where someone ran through the room with a letter-opener covered in blood or a pen covered in grease. Some participants did recall the details of the high-stress condition better, but this wasn't true for all participants.

> *ℓ* The candidate has produced the findings from just two studies but given both of them in reasonable detail. The interpretation offered for the first study (explaining why recall in the UK is evidence of flashbulb memory) is a conclusion rather than a finding. For full marks we are looking for more details (for example, the candidate could have included the names of the researchers) or more findings. The material presented here does not focus sufficiently on findings. (4 out of 6 marks)

(c) Loftus has conducted a lot of research into eyewitness testimony. In one study (Loftus and Palmer) participants were shown clips of an automobile accident and asked to say how fast the car was travelling. Their estimate of the speed was affected by the words that had been used to describe the accident. So if the word 'smashed into' was used, the participants suggested a much faster speed than if the words 'hit each other' were used. This suggests that eyewitness reports might be affected by the way the eyewitnesses are questioned.

In another study by Loftus the participants were asked a question about a headlight. If the question was changed so that participants were asked about 'the' broken headlight, more of them remembered the headlight than when it was just 'a' broken headlight (in fact there was no headlight). This shows the effect of language again.

In a similar study, Loftus arranged for participants to watch a film of a car travelling through the countryside. They were all asked how fast a white sports car was travelling but some of them were asked the question with '...as it passed the barn' (but there was no barn). Later, when participants were asked if they saw a barn in the film those who had been prompted to think there might have been a barn were more likely to report that they saw it.

> *ℓ* This candidate has described a number of studies in considerable detail and is rewarded with good AO1 marks (5 out of 6), though the material selected is somewhat limited, almost as if Loftus's research is the only information the candidate knows about eyewitness testimony. However, the key problem is that minimal use has been made of this material, thus attracting few AO2 marks. There are a few comments, such as at the end of the first paragraph. An AO2 mark of 2 out of 12 would be appropriate here, making a total of 7 out of 18 marks.

Total for this question: 17 out of 30 marks

Answer to question 2: candidate B

(a) STM, as the name suggests, has a short duration and a limited capacity. Research has found that memories in STM last between 15 and 30 seconds. LTM memory is affected by forgetting but some memories there do appear to last for ever, especially those related to episodic memory. STM has a limited capacity. This means that as new information enters, this can interfere with information there and lead to forgetting in STM. This is less true of LTM which has a potentially infinite capacity. There is a third difference between the two stores which is in terms of the way that material is likely to be forgotten. Because STM is a limited capacity store of short duration, forgetting tends to be due to interference or decay. In LTM, explanations for forgetting are most likely to be related to lack of accessibility rather than availability.

e This answer is clearly more thorough than the one given by the first candidate but gets no extra marks. This candidate has perhaps used examination time carelessly and could suffer later. (6 out of 6 marks)

(b) Rubin and Kozin (1984) found that people reported significant events, such as their first romance. Bohannon found that the accuracy of eyewitness accounts of the Challenger space disaster fell from 77% to 55% over 8 months, suggesting that flashbulb memories were not very accurate. Conway et al. thought that this was because the event didn't have that much emotional significance. Conway et al. found that people in the UK had better recall for events surrounding the resignation of Mrs Thatcher than people in other countries, showing that with greater emotional significance flashbulb memory was better than normal memory.

e This is an excellent collection of relevant findings (plus some other details that don't attract credit), all accurate and detailed. (6 out of 6 marks)

(c) Research evidence abounds with studies that have demonstrated how eyewitness testimony can be unreliable.

First of all there is the issue of how the language used in questioning a potential eyewitness can affect what they remember. Loftus showed that using 'the' rather than 'a' when asking a question can mislead a participant into thinking that something actually existed when it didn't. The person asking the question might use 'a' or 'the' depending on their own expectations, but this would influence the eyewitness.

A second problem for eyewitness testimony is the accuracy of recall. Lots of memory research shows that we recall things rather poorly and in fact we tend to reconstruct our memories on the basis of past experience. This was Bartlett's view of memory, and was supported by his own research into the way people recollected information that was unfamiliar to them (e.g. the 'War of the Ghosts'). A study by Allport and Postman (1947) also showed how people tended to remember a knife in a Black man's hand rather than the White man he was arguing with (in fact the knife was in the White man's hand). This shows that people's recall is influenced by their expectations and would tend to make it unreliable.

Another issue, related to unreliability, that is worth considering is the effects of emotion on recall. On the one hand there is evidence that extremely emotional events can enhance memory (flashbulb memories), but equally there is evidence that disturbing events are repressed. This is a difficult area of research because of the ethics of exposing participants to emotionally traumatic events.

Finally, one might consider how good people are at face recognition. Studies of face recognition show that we use cues about faces in motion rather than actual individual features (Bruce and Valentine, 1988) and this would suggest that photofit images are not very useful or reliable ways of trying to identify criminals.

Psychological research is useful in suggesting ways to increase the reliability of eyewitness testimony, such as the use of context-dependent recall.

e This response illustrates how an answer can be organised in terms of arguments rather than using research studies as the backbone and then stating what they show. Here the candidate has answered the question repeatedly, for example stating that memory research shows that EWT can be affected by language and lacks accuracy, and then supporting this statement with reference to research. AO1 marks are gained through the description of such research, which is both accurate and detailed (6 out of 6 marks). AO2 credit is gained through the analysis of the question (breaking it down into various sub-arguments) and other commentary, such as on ethics. There is substantial evidence that the candidate's opinion is informed by psychological evidence and this knowledge has been used effectively, for 11 out of 12 marks. Some of the points might perhaps have been more thoroughly explained. This makes a total of 17 out of 18 marks.

Total for this question: 29 out of 30 marks

Cognitive psychology (III)

(a) **Explain the concepts of repression and flashbulb memory.** (3 + 3 marks)

(b) **Describe the working memory model.** (6 marks)

(c) **'Some psychologists have been highly critical of traditional memory research because of its focus on theoretical issues and a lack of interest in more practical topics.'**

Evaluate the practical usefulness of memory research, for example in terms of eyewitness testimony. (18 marks)

Total: 30 marks

(a) In order to explain a concept you need to define it, but in addition to this, you should make the implications of the definition clear. Therefore, you might also use examples to elucidate your explanation. At the end you want to write something that would make the concept clear to someone with no psychological knowledge.

(b) Another straightforward and predictable question. You might find it helpful to use a diagram as part of your description, but don't let that stand alone. Demonstrate that you haven't simply memorised the diagram but that you understand the meaning of the different components and the overall usefulness of the model. Don't include any evaluation as that is not required by this part of the question.

(c) How useful is memory research? What do you think? This is the question you are aiming to answer. You might make reference specifically to studies of eyewitness testimony or you might consider any studies of memory in terms of how their findings could be practically applied — not least to the problems that are immediately facing you of how to remember material for an examination! What, for example, can levels of processing research tell you about studying and revising? As before, focus more on the question asked and use your knowledge to present an *informed* argument, rather than devoting the whole essay to a description of research. Strike a balance between describing research studies and using them to support your argument.

■ ■ ■

Answer to question 3: candidate A

(a) Repression is forgetting something that is unpleasant. A flashbulb memory is an accurate memory of something, like a picture.

Both definitions are generally accurate, though rather basic. Neither explanation quite makes it to 2 marks because of the vague terminology used. The answer would have been improved simply by using more precise words instead of 'something'. (2 out of 6 marks)

(b) The working memory model refers to that part of memory that is active when you are working on something. It is equivalent to short-term memory. But Baddeley and Hitch suggested that you could further divide short-term memory into other stores such as one that deals with visual data and another that deals with acoustic data. Both are coordinated by the central executive.

> *e* The candidate has a grasp of the model but lacks the details. The answer would have been significantly improved by using the correct terms such as 'visuo-spatial scratchpad' and 'phonological loop'. In the model the phonological loop is further sub-divided, so there is more detail that has been omitted here. (3 out of 6 marks — the answer is generally accurate but lacking detail.)

(c) A lot of memory research takes place in laboratories and involves giving lists of words to participants. For example, the interference experiments are very unlike anything we do in real life and therefore only tell us about laboratory memory. They can't give us advice on how to improve our memories.

An important area where memory research might be useful is in eyewitness testimony, but here again the studies are carried out in laboratories. For example, the study by Loftus where participants were asked if they saw 'a broken headlight' or 'the broken headlight' showed that using the word 'a' or 'the' made a difference to the answer given by the participants. There was in fact no broken headlight but the participants given 'the' were more likely to answer 'yes'. This is evidence of misleading questions which might be used, unwittingly, by a policeman interviewing a potential witness, or by a lawyer in court.

But since this evidence was gathered in a laboratory, does it tell us about real life? In this case the answer might be 'yes' but, on the other hand, in real life, people are more certain about what they know or don't know and aren't responding to the experimenter's demand characteristics. So maybe the answer is 'no'.

Another kind of study that has been done by psychologists is to look at flashbulb memories and see if they really exist. It is difficult to study this in a laboratory because it means you have to make someone experience an intense emotion. Therefore we have to use case studies or ask people what they can recall, for example, about the day that Princess Diana died. If we do this, then we have no way of confirming how accurate their answers are.

> *e* The answer starts quite well, and the candidate considers two examples of memory research which may or may not be applicable to real life. The candidate has used the guidance in the question to focus on eyewitness testimony but has also considered other areas of memory research — which is quite acceptable. The issue about why laboratory research might be artificial is touched upon (there might be demand characteristics), which is excellent and thoughtful. The last paragraph is not made relevant to the question but there is the potential for an interesting commentary — that some research might be of greater practical usefulness but would lack control. In this case, however, we would say that the candidate has not used the material effectively. Overall, the candidate has made a reasonable attempt to answer the question set and to try to focus on analysis

and commentary, but not always with success. The efforts of engaging with the material has meant overlooking AO1 material — there is little descriptive content here (2 out of 6 marks), but a reasonable, though limited, commentary (8 out of 12 marks). This makes a total of 10 out of 18 marks.

Total for this question: 15 out of 30 marks

■ ■ ■

Answer to question 3: candidate B

(a) Both of these are forms of forgetting that can be linked to emotion. Repression occurs when a thought or memory creates anxiety. One's ego defends itself by repressing the thought and making it inaccessible. A flashbulb memory is an accurate and long-lasting memory that is formed at a time of intense emotion. It might concern significant public or personal events.

> *e* Both definitions are accurate and detailed, though the second one lacks clarity, so is given 2 out of 3 marks. It is important to be clear that a flashbulb memory concerns the context in which the event was experienced and not the event itself. (5 out of 6 marks)

(b) Baddeley and Hitch (1974) proposed that short-term memory is more accurately represented in terms of a set of separate stores which handle different modalities (sound and visual data) rather than a single store, as in the multi-store model. The use of the term 'working memory' reflects the idea that this is the area of memory that is active when you are working on information. Working memory consists of: a central executive (the modality-free organiser), a phonological loop (verbal material) and a visuo-spatial sketchpad (visual memories). The phonological loop is further subdivided into a phonological store (speech perception) and an articulatory process (speech production). According to this model we can do two tasks at one time if they involve different stores because each task involves a different modality, whereas we have trouble with tasks that might both involve the same store.

> *e* Again, the candidate provides an answer that is detailed and accurate. This is probably more detailed than would be expected in the 5–6 minutes available for this answer. (6 out of 6 marks)

(c) There are many ways in which memory research is, or could be, useful. Perhaps the most obvious way is in eyewitness testimony. Court cases often hang on such testimony and psychological research has been very important in showing in what way such evidence is unreliable.

First of all, what a person thinks they saw is likely to be influenced by their past experiences and expectations. A study by Cohen showed that when people watched a video of a woman and were later asked questions about what she was doing, their answers were influenced by whether they had been told before watching the video that she was a waitress or a librarian. The recall of what she did was in line with the expectations generated by her stereotype. This suggests that if you saw a Black man at the scene of a crime you might be more likely to think that the person was involved than if it was a little old lady. In fact one study by Postman and Allport showed this most strongly. Participants were asked to describe a picture they were shown. There was a White man and a Black man on a subway train, and the White man was holding a knife. However, most people recalled that it was the Black man holding the knife.

A second kind of evidence from psychological research has indicated how the words that are used shape what you remember. In a classic study by Carmichael et al. (1930s), participants were shown line pictures and given words to describe them. One group of participants was given one list and the other group was given a second list. For example, they were shown a lozenge shape and told that it was either a kidney bean or a canoe. Their later recall was like the descriptive term that was used. For example, if the drawing was described as a kidney bean, it was likely to look like this. Research by Loftus has also shown how language affects memory. In one study the word 'smashed' led participants to estimate higher speeds than if the word 'hit' was used to describe a car accident. In another study, participants were shown a film and asked a question about a person driving past a barn (though in the original film there was no barn). Later, when participants were asked about the barn, those who had been asked the question were more likely to recall wrongly a barn. In real life there was an incident involving some people working in a garage at the time of the Oklahoma bombing. One of them reported two men and so the police tried to find two men. When the other garage workers heard this, they too started to think that there were two men. In fact there was only one man, but what you hear others saying might make you think that is what you saw (like the barn).

> 🖉 The candidate has focused entirely on eyewitness testimony, which is perfectly legitimate, and located some useful evidence to support the arguments. However, there is rather too much description of this evidence, which means less time being available to explore the arguments more thoroughly, and so less credit for analysis. The answer focuses on the limitations highlighted by memory research without exploring positive recommendations that might be made. Even though there is no requirement to present a balanced view, such an approach is desirable. Finally, at the end of the essay it is not clear whether the candidate has effectively considered the question of the practical usefulness of memory research (is it useful?). Instead the answer ends with material related to the reliability of eyewitness testimony. It reads somewhat like a 'prepared' answer. Full marks are awarded for AO1 (6 out of 6 marks) but the commentary is basic; it would be judged as rudimentary except for the way the AO1 material has sometimes been used effectively (5 out of 12 marks), making a total of 11 out of 18 marks.

Total for this question: 22 out of 30 marks

Q4

Cognitive psychology (IV)

(a) Outline *two* explanations of forgetting in long-term memory.   (3+3 marks)

(b) Outline findings of *one* study of memory for faces and give one criticism
of this study.   (3+3 marks)

(c) 'The ultimate aim of conducting psychological investigations is to test the
theories constructed by psychologists.'
To what extent does research evidence support the multi-store model
of memory?   (18 marks)

Total: 30 marks

(a) This question starts, like many others, with a relatively straightforward description/
explanation of terms taken directly from the specification. You should have little
trouble with these because you should know they are likely to come up. The
difficulty perhaps lies in ensuring that you write enough for 3 marks. You must
name each explanation and then communicate your understanding of how this
explanation does account for long-term forgetting.

(b) This part of the question is split into two equal halves, as indicated by the marks
(3+3). For the first half you should describe one or more findings from one study
of memory for faces. One finding would be sufficient for maximum marks if it is
provided in enough detail. Remember that you have about 3 minutes for this, which
should indicate the kind of detail required. The same principle applies to your
criticism. Ensure that the criticism is relevant to the study.

(c) There is a danger that you will simply use this question to describe all the studies
you know on encoding, capacity and duration of short- and long-term memory. But
that is not what the question requires. It asks you to consider *to what extent* such
research supports the model. Ideally, you should consider evidence that does
support the model and whether this evidence is sound. You then need to consider
evidence that does not support the model, and the soundness of this evidence.
Finally, you might reach some conclusion in answer to the question. When
considering supporting evidence you might group the studies in terms of the way
they support different aspects of the model (e.g. verbal rehearsal and separate
stores). You have just 15 minutes, so do try to avoid describing the studies in too
much detail — especially the procedures.

■ ■ ■

Answer to question 4: candidate A

(a) A person might forget something from long-term memory because of cue-
dependent forgetting. This means that a memory is available but not accessible
because you don't have the right cue to access it. Another explanation for forgetting in long-term memory is interference.

question

📝 The first explanation is accurate and fairly detailed but it lacks clarity and therefore receives 2 marks. The second explanation is basic. It is not clear that the candidate understands this explanation at all, so just 1 mark is given here. (3 out of 6 marks)

(b) One study of memory for faces involved showing people faces in motion, except all that the participants could see were the shadows that suggested motion. The researchers found that participants were able to identify various different facial expressions, such as whether the face was smiling or frowning. They could even identify some people on the basis of movement only. The main criticism of this study was that it was conducted in a laboratory and might not apply to real life.

📝 The candidate begins with material not relevant to this question as it relates to the procedures and not the findings of the study. The detail in the answer would have been enhanced by naming the study (Bruce and Valentine, 1988), but this doesn't detract from the detail provided in relation to the findings. This is accurate and gains 3 marks. The one criticism, however, is minimal. It is not clear whether this is or is not a problem in this particular study, but as it was a laboratory study, the criticism would receive 1 mark for peripheral relevance. (4 out of 6 marks)

(c) There are lots of studies that support the multi-store model. For example, the study by Peterson and Peterson showed that short-term memory has restricted capacity because the longer that participants had to wait before recalling trigrams, the more they forgot. The duration of STM is about 15 seconds. Another study by Bahrick et al. showed that long-term memory lasts for a very long time. This supports the multi-store model.

The study by Glanzer and Cunitz showed that when participants had to recall word lists there was a primacy and recency effect. The primacy effect occurs because the first words have gone into long-term memory and can be recalled better, and the recency effect occurs because the last words are still in the short-term store.

Research on brain damage also supports the existence of two different stores. KF had an intact long-term memory but couldn't recall anything new that happened since his motorbike accident.

There is also evidence for a third sensory store. Sperling showed that participants could recall a higher percentage of data if asked to recall just one row of letters/numbers, whereas if they had to report all the data, the percentage recall fell, presumably because the data disappeared from the sensory store during the time it took to recall the data. This is not included in any of the other models.

📝 This candidate has made a good effort to answer the question set. A number of relevant studies are described in appropriate detail, though perhaps not quite enough for full marks (5 out of 6 marks). There are a number of attempts to use the evidence effectively as part of an argument about the multi-store model, but some of these (e.g. 'this supports the multi-store model') are not very informative. Furthermore, the candidate really needs to go beyond the actual studies and consider the value of this evidence. For example, are there alternative ways that the data could be interpreted, such as within levels of processing theory? Are there criticisms that might be made of this kind of research on explicit memory tested in laboratory conditions? The commentary is reasonably effective but basic. However, it is closer to limited than superficial (thus 6 out of 12 marks). This makes a total of 11 out of 18 marks.

Total for this question: 18 out of 30 marks

■ ■ ■

Answer to question 4: candidate B

(a) Long-term forgetting might be due to decay, in other words, material that was once in memory disappears through disuse. Research into cue-dependent recall suggests that this might be rare. Clearly, some kinds of memories, such as riding a bicycle, never decay. If you can't remember something it could be because it was never well stored in memory in the first place. The second explanation is retrieval failure, or cue-dependent recall. The reason one can't recall something from long-term memory (and therefore it appears forgotten) is that one does not have an appropriate retrieval cue. Research (e.g. by Tulving) shows that the words are there and can be retrieved when the person is given an appropriate cue.

    e Both explanations are detailed and accurate, though the first one could be clearer. The candidate is trying to say that decay is not a good explanation for forgetting in memory — but it is still an explanation. (6 out of 6 marks)

(b) One study of memory for faces is by Yin et al. They combined the top half of one person's face with the bottom half of another and asked participants to recognise both contributing faces. Participants found it harder to recognise the two contributing faces when the top half and bottom half were closely aligned, presumably because the close alignment produced a new configuration. One criticism of this study is that other research has shown that motion is more important in face recognition and this study only tested recognition of a still face. On the other hand, this study is relevant to what happens in Identikit photo recognition.

    e The candidate has provided details of other aspects of the study, not just findings, for the first part of this question. What is given is worth 2 out of 3 marks (generally accurate but limited detail). The criticism offered is well elaborated and appropriate. It is clearly linked to the particular study rather than being a criticism of research in general, so it receives 3 out of 3 marks. (5 out of 6 marks)

(c) The multi-store model proposes that memory consists of three separate stores: sensory, short-term and long-term stores. Material is passed from one store to the next through verbal rehearsal. If data are not rehearsed, they decay.

The sensory store is demonstrated in Sperling's research, where participants were able to remember a higher percentage of data if they only had to recall one out of three rows. The reason for this is that if they had to recall all three rows, the data had decayed before they were able to recall them. So data must be passed from the eyes and ears to short-term memory to avoid rapid decay. This demonstrates the first (sensory) store.

A lot of studies show that there are two qualitatively different stores after sensory memory: one that has limited capacity and duration (short-term store); and another that is potentially for ever (long-term store). For example, it would be hard to explain the serial position effect without reference to STM and LTM. The effect describes how, when recalling a list of words, participants typically can best remember the first words and the last words in the list. These are called the primacy and recency effects respectively. These occur because the words from the beginning of the list have been passed to LTM and the words at the end of the list are still in STM, so both first and last words are more easily recalled than the middle words (Glanzer and Cunitz).

Case studies of individuals with brain damage, like HM and KF, show that they had intact long-term memories but could not hold anything in the immediate memory, nor could they form new long-term memories. This only makes sense in terms of separate stores.

However, there is other research, such as Craik and Lockhart's study of processing words at shallow and deep levels, that cannot be explained in terms of this model. The multi-store model also cannot explain studies of implicit memory where participants have been able to recall data even though they had not been told to remember the words. For example, Mandler asked participants to sort packs of word cards into categories repeatedly and later surprised the participants with a test asking them to recall the words on the cards. They would not have been verbally rehearsing the words but still were able to recall most of them. The categorisation required by the task meant they processed the material deeply.

A further problem with the multi-store model is that the data are exclusively from laboratory studies of memory and therefore might only apply to a particular kind of memory, and not other things like remembering how to ride a bicycle.

e There is a nice balance to this essay — the first half aims to indicate how the multi-store model is supported by research evidence and the second half looks at studies that do not support the model plus other issues that challenge the model (such as the kind of research conducted). There is a nice variety in the commentary offered. The descriptive content is kept to the background to ensure there is sufficient AO2 content. A good range of research is described accurately and sufficiently for full marks (6 out of 6). The commentary is reasonably thorough. It is effective because all the description is linked seamlessly with stating what the material shows. This is enough for full marks (12 out of 12), making a total of 18 out of 18 marks.

Total for this question: 29 out of 30 marks

Developmental psychology (I)

(a) **Outline the development of attachments.** (6 marks)

(b) **Describe the procedures and findings of *one* study of individual differences in attachment.** (6 marks)

(c) **'Day-care provision is seen as beneficial for the cognitive development of some children whereas it is argued that the same provision may harm the child's social development.'**
To what extent does day-care have positive effects on cognitive and/or social development? (18 marks)

Total: 30 marks

(a) The term 'outline' is used here instead of 'describe' because you only have 6 minutes to write about the development of attachments. You are not going to be able to provide much specific detail, but just sketch out the various stages/ phases that have been identified in the way an infant's attachments change over time (i.e. in terms of different stages rather than details of each stage).

(b) You do not need to provide an answer that is balanced in terms of procedures and findings, but do ensure that you include both procedures and findings and do not include details of aims and conclusions, or any other aspect of the study. It increases the 'detail' to name the study and to give the date. Neither is strictly necessary, but they are desirable.

(c) This part of the question requires analysis and commentary as well as description. Ensure you avoid a focus on the descriptions of research studies. Instead, the intention is that you should use such material *effectively*. For example, you might identify and describe briefly a study on how day-care affects cognitive development, but in order to use this effectively you must state what the study tells us about the effects of day-care on cognitive development. The best approach in answering this question is first of all to consider what arguments you might present, for example 'day-care is detrimental to social and cognitive development', and 'day-care is not detrimental to social and cognitive development'. For each, consider a few studies that support your argument. Finally, present a conclusion — not just a summary of the points made, but a genuine conclusion and about what the research indicates. Note that the question says cognitive and/or social development, so you can use evidence relating to either or to both.

■ ■ ■

Answer to question 5: candidate A

(a) The first stage in the development of attachments is when infants are happy to be held by anyone. They don't cry when they are left and don't really know the difference between people and other objects. Later they become specially attached to one person; they cry if this person leaves them and are happy when they see the person again.

> 🖉 The candidate has expressed some understanding of the development of attachments and has focused on two important features: (1) the departure of an attachment object is a sign of the development of attachment; and (2) attachments become specific. However, much information has been omitted (such as the approximate age when specific attachments form). (2 out of 6 marks — the answer is not muddled or flawed but is lacking in detail and fairly basic.)

(b) Ainsworth studied individual differences in attachment in the Strange Situation experiment. Infants were placed in a room with their mother and then were left on their own, or left just with a stranger. The experimenter observed what the infant did when left alone and also when the mother came back. The findings were that some children were securely attached (about 65%) because they didn't object much when their mothers left and were happy to see them back again. Other children were quite distressed when their mother left and ignored her when she came back. This is called insecure attachment.

> 🖉 The answer covers both procedures and findings. The procedures could have been described much more exactly and are best described as basic. More detail is provided for the findings. The candidate provides a percentage which, while not exactly right, does indicate some knowledge of the study (Ainsworth and Bell found that 71% were securely attached) and details of two different kinds of behaviour that were observed. (4 out of 6 marks — the descriptions of procedures and findings are generally accurate, but limited.

(c) The Headstart study gave working-class children day-care provision, with the intention of increasing their cognitive abilities before they went to school. This was carried out because some children might fail in school because they start off at a disadvantage. The study found that the children's IQs were increased after attending day-care where there was a special emphasis on cognitive development.

Other studies have looked at the effects of day-care on social development because Bowlby thought that if a child was separated from his or her mother, then the child would be emotionally damaged by this separation. This led some people to think that day-care might not be good for children.

Then what about the Headstart children? They might have had higher IQs but been emotionally damaged. In fact recent research shows that children who go to day-care are OK socially and emotionally.

So it seems that day-care has no negative effects on the social and cognitive development of the child. In fact it might have positive effects. Another study conducted in Sweden found that infants who had been in day-care from a very early age actually had higher IQs than children who had not attended day-care. One reason for this might be because day-care is of a very high quality in Sweden. Perhaps the reason why day-care sometimes has negative effects is because the ratio of staff to infants is poor, so the children don't really get as much attention as they would at home. In this case the children who are at home with their mothers do better.

> ℮ The main task in this extended answer is to avoid too much description (maximum of 6 marks) and focus on evaluating the issue raised (maximum of 12 marks), in this case the question of whether day-care has positive or negative effects on cognitive and/or social development. This candidate has provided a brief but effective response. There is some breadth (dealing with both cognitive and social development) and there is balance (both positive and negative effects are considered). The material has been used in a reasonably effective manner, though some arguments might have been more clearly elaborated (slightly limited analysis). The commentary cannot be fairly described as informed as the references used are rather vague and limited in scope (really only two pieces of research). The descriptive content could have been stronger and suggests a lack of familiarity with the details of the studies (3 out of 6 marks), but this is balanced by a good mark for evaluation, as this is what the candidate has focused on (9 out of 12 marks). This makes a total of 12 out of 18 marks.

Total for this question: 18 out of 30 marks

■ ■ ■

Answer to question 5: candidate B

(a) The first phase is called 'pre-attachment', when infants are responsive to anyone and anything. They do recognise special individuals but they are also quite happy to be held by anyone. By the age of about 2 months, infants show clearer recognition of a primary caregiver. They continue to be relatively easily comforted by anyone, and do not yet show anxiety with strangers. Around the age of 7 months, infants typically show two signs of specific attachments: separation protest and stranger anxiety. Both of these indicate that the infant is specially reliant and attached to one specific person who is best able to comfort the individual. This also demonstrates an increased ability to discriminate between individuals because now the child feels anxious about strangers. Very soon after the main attachment is formed, the infant develops a wider circle of attachments depending on how many consistent relationships he/she has.

> ℮ It would be hard to fault this answer given the time constraint. The candidate has produced an accurate and detailed response which is probably more than one might reasonably expect in 6 minutes. (6 out of 6 marks)

(b) A classic study by Shaffer and Emerson (1964) documented the early development of infants in Glasgow. Their method was to visit the infants' homes on a regular basis over a 2 year period, and ask the mothers about the infants' behaviour. For example, they asked the mothers to say how the babies behaved if they were left alone in a room or when they were put down after being held

question

by an adult. This meant they could assess separation anxiety at each visit. They also noted down how the infant behaved towards the researchers, which showed stranger anxiety. Schaffer and Emerson found that most infants had developed specific attachments by the age of 8 months and shortly thereafter had developed attachments with other family members. By 18 months only 13% were attached to only one person.

> It is reasonable to choose this study instead of the more obvious Strange Situation, if the candidate knows the kind of detail provided above. The candidate has provided details about both procedures and findings, and the findings are related to individual differences (most, but not all, infants had developed attachments). The study did provide other findings on individual differences, for example that some infants were more intensely attached than others. (6 out of 6 marks — findings and procedures are covered. Detailed and accurate.)

(c) There are many potential effects of day-care, but the two most important ones are in terms of cognitive and social development. The view that day-care can have negative effects on social development stems from Bowlby's maternal deprivation hypothesis which stated that infants who have frequent separations from their primary caregiver are likely to experience permanent emotional damage. This would suggest that being in day-care would be undesirable. However, a variety of research studies have not found this to be the case. For example, Kagan et al. (1980) compared infants in a special day-care centre with those raised at home and found no large differences between the groups. On the other hand, a study of childminders in London (Mayall and Petrie) did find some disturbing effects when comparing the children being childminded with those who spent the time at home.

It is possible to explain these findings in terms of the kind of care being received. In the nursery the children had a lot of attention whereas the child-minding study found that some childminders actually gave the children rather little attention and rewarded them for being undemanding and quiet. This is supported by a study in Sweden by Andersson (1992) where the children in day-care actually did better in school than those not in day-care. In Sweden day-care is well funded by the government and of a high quality.

Another study, in the States, found that children in low-quality day-care were less secure. They also found that if an infant's mother lacked responsiveness, then the child did less well in a care situation. So it might not be the day-care itself but the fact that the child's home provided poor emotional support that is significant. A further study, by Egeland and Hiester (1995), found that day-care had a positive influence on insecurely attached children. This is a bit at odds with the other finding, but does indicate that day-care can affect children differently.

In terms of cognitive development, the child's emotional development might be important. The development of IQ could be held back if a child is emotionally insecure, and children who do not interact well with their carers won't develop as quickly. Therefore, if day-care promotes social and emotional development, then this should not restrict cognitive development.

Another angle to consider is the fact that children in day-care learn to interact better with their peers and might arrive at school better able to cope with the pressures of having to interact with other children. Those children who spent their infancy at home might find the school environment rather a shock and this could delay their academic progress. On the other hand, there could be individual differences here as well. Pennebaker et al. (1981) found that shy children found the day-care experience threatening and did not thrive.

There is no simple answer to the question of whether day-care has positive or negative effects.

e The candidate has managed to cover a considerable amount of material in the time allocated. The answer receives credit for the extent to which it is informed — a number of research studies have been effectively used to discuss both positive and negative effects on social and cognitive development. They are accurately referenced and described in sufficient detail for the full AO1 marks (6 out of 6). The argument is balanced and quite thorough (12 out 12 marks), making a total of 18 out of 18 marks.

Total for this question: 30 out of 30 marks

Developmental psychology (II)

(a) Define the terms 'attachment', 'deprivation' and 'privation' in relation to
child development. (2+2+2 marks)

(b) Outline findings of research into the effects of deprivation and/or separation. (6 marks)

(c) 'Bowlby claimed that children who experience early and lasting separations
from their primary attachment figure will experience later emotional
maladjustment.'

Consider the extent to which Bowlby's claim has been supported by research
evidence related to privation. (18 marks)

Total: 30 marks

(a) Try to be concise when answering this type of question. If you are struggling to get
your meaning across succinctly, try adding an example to show the examiner that
you know what you are talking about. A sentence or two will normally suffice for
such definitions. Check your understanding of these terms against the definitions
provided on pages 37 and 38.

(b) You must focus on findings only. 'Research' can include theories as well as studies,
so you might report the 'findings' of a theory. The more findings you can cover,
the more marks you will attract. This could be in terms of multiple findings from
one study and/or various findings from different studies. Two findings would be
sufficient for full marks if given in enough detail. Material on privation would be
creditworthy.

(c) Don't forget that in this part of the question you must resist the temptation to
describe research studies. Your aim is to *use* such studies to support your
argument. This inevitably involves some description, but you need to make sure
that you offer twice as much evaluation. You are required to offer your opinion but
this opinion must be informed, i.e. make reference to psychological research. In this
question you should consider research evidence that does support Bowlby's
maternal deprivation hypothesis and also research evidence that suggests that
Bowlby's claim was flawed. In the case of both lines of argument, you might further
consider the soundness of the research evidence itself. Note that the question
refers to privation only, though you might include material on deprivation as a
means of highlighting the significance of privation.

■ ■ ■

Answer to question 6: candidate A

(a) Attachment is the bond between an infant and its caregiver. Deprivation is the
loss of attachments, whereas privation is the lack of attachments.

*All three definitions are correct, but none of them has been given in sufficient detail
for 2 marks — thus they are each worth 1 mark. (3 out of 6 marks)*

(b) One study that has looked at short-term separation was by Robertson and Robertson. They observed and filmed various children who experienced brief separations from their parents. The children displayed the stages of separation protest: protest, despair and finally detachment. In the case of two of the girls the Robertsons looked after them in their home and allowed the girls to bring things with them from home and to talk about their mother. These girls appeared to be quite well adjusted and coped well.

> The candidate hasn't quite answered the question, providing information about the procedures of the studies rather than focusing on findings alone. There is little information about the findings. (2 out of 6 marks — basic.)

(c) One area of research into privation has used case studies of children who have had extremely difficult early childhoods. Genie, for example, spent her early years locked up in a room and tied to a chair. At the age of 12 she was discovered and spent her later years looked after by another family. She never quite recovered from her early ordeal, though there might be explanations for this. Her father said he locked her away because she was retarded from birth, and therefore her poor recovery might be because she was never quite right. Another issue is that her mother claimed that, even though Genie was locked away, she had had a relationship with her daughter. This highlights the problems of a retrospective case study — one can never be sure exactly what the child's experiences were.

Perhaps better evidence can be gained from looking at a longitudinal study by Tizard and Hodges. The children in this study spent their early lives in an institution. Some of them were adopted while others went back to their original homes. Bowlby said that it is better to be in one's own home than in an institution, but in fact the children who returned home did less well at school than those who remained in the institution. However, this makes sense when one considers that these children were going back to situations that had been less than ideal in the first place.

Other children who have been in institutional care, such as Romanian orphans, have been shown not to do well. However, their poor progress might be due to general deprivation rather than just the lack of attachments.

> This answer uses research evidence from studies and Bowlby's theory ('Bowlby said it is better to be in one's own home...'). The information is accurate but not always as detailed as it could be. Against this we must balance the variety of evidence described (4 out of 6 marks). This evidence has been used in a reasonably effective manner to answer the question and additional useful comments are offered, such as 'This highlights the problems of a retrospective case study'. The material used clearly relates to privation rather than deprivation, as required. It is perhaps better described as limited rather than slightly limited (7 out of 12 marks). This makes a total of 11 out of 18 marks.

Total for this question: 16 out of 30 marks

Answer to question 6: candidate B

(a) Attachment is an emotional tie between an infant and a caregiver that results in a desire to maintain proximity. Deprivation is the loss of contact with an attachment figure after attachments have been formed. Privation occurs when there has been no opportunity for any bond to develop, i.e. the complete lack of any attachment.

e All three definitions are accurate and detailed. (6 out of 6 marks)

(b) Bowlby studied children who experienced frequent separations from their families, and found that these children later were more likely to become juvenile delinquents and could be characterised as 'affectionless psychopaths', whereas the same was not true of children who didn't experience early separations. These children might also become disturbed (for other reasons), but they did not become affectionless psychopaths. A study by Rutter also looked at early separations and found that it was the discord in children's homes rather than the separations which was linked to maladjustment.

e The candidate has reported a number of appropriate findings, fairly accurately and with reasonable detail. The detail is perhaps not quite enough for full marks. For full marks the candidate might have emphasised the actual findings more clearly, as required by the question. (5 out of 6 marks)

(c) Research on privation has included case studies which tend to offer weak evidence because we cannot be certain what early experiences the children had. For example, in the case of the Koluchová twins, even though they clearly experienced extreme early deprivation after being locked in a cupboard, they did have each other — and they did recover reasonably well. Those individuals, such as Genie, who were truly isolated, did not recover, but we cannot know whether or not they were normal from the beginning.

Better evidence comes from the study of the effects of institutional care. In Tizard and Hodges's research, those children who were adopted into good homes showed good relationships within their families at age 16, despite early privation. The children who had returned to their original homes did not have good relationships. This suggests that it is possible to recover from early privation, except that both groups of children found peer relationships at school difficult. The interpretation is that the privated children were OK in relationships where others were working hard on their behalf but, with peers, they lacked the emotional ability to conduct normal healthy relationships. So this suggests that early privation does have an effect, which supports Bowlby.

Recent research has considered the development of Romanian orphans who were adopted in the UK (Rutter et al.). When these children were first adopted they were very much behind their peers in the UK, but by the age of 4 they had caught up. However, it is significant that age at adoption was negatively correlated with attainment of developmental milestones. In other words, the later the children were adopted, the slower their progress. So this suggests that the longer children experience emotional deprivation, the longer it will take for them to recover.

Other research by Rutter, with Quinton, found that institutionalised women were worse parents later in life, which suggests that early privation did affect their ability to form relationships as adults.

An excellent range of research evidence is described, and in good detail (6 out of 6 marks). This material is introduced effectively in relation to certain arguments (e.g. 'Research on privation has included case studies which tend to offer weak evidence...for example...') which inform the reader about what kind of support there is for Bowlby and the value of this support. There are persistent attempts to draw out conclusions ('This suggests that...') and offer commentary ('However, it is significant that...'). This is an informed commentary and a reasonably thorough analysis, though it lacks balance because it focuses mainly on support. This is not a requirement of the question, but should be the aim of a top essay (11 out of 12 marks). This makes a total of 17 out of 18 marks.

Total for this question: 28 out of 30 marks

Developmental psychology (III)

(a) **What is meant by the terms 'secure attachment' and 'insecure attachment'?** (3 + 3 marks)

(b) **Outline *one* explanation of attachment (e.g. Bowlby).** (6 marks)

(c) **'One problem with any theory of attachment is that it suggests that all children develop in similar ways all over the world.'**
To what extent do cross-cultural variations affect the development of attachment? (18 marks)

Total: 30 marks

(a) The two definitions are worth 3 marks each rather than 2, which reflects the fact that there is a significant amount you can write about them. It is not simply a matter of definition but an elaboration of what is implied by these terms. You might consider the way the different behaviours are expressed in the Strange Situation and/or the effects on subsequent development.

(b) The fact that the term 'outline' is used suggests that you are likely to have a lot of information you could use to answer this question. However, the maximum mark is only 6 and this offers you guidance about the amount of time you should spend. The term 'outline' advises you to stick to the essential details of the theory rather than feeling you have to provide more information. Note that you can outline any theory of attachment. Bowlby is given only as an example. You should also note that if you do describe Bowlby's theory, his theory of attachment is different from his maternal deprivation hypothesis, though there are overlaps.

(c) If you are unsure how to answer this question, use the quote to give you some idea where to begin. In what ways do theories of attachment suggest that all children are similar? What does research in other countries suggest about attachment? Are there variations in different cultures, or even in sub-cultures within one country? You might try to generate your own questions and use them to give you ideas about what to discuss. In essence, you are aiming to consider how differences in various cultures are related to differences in attachment — or is attachment the same all over the world? Resist, as far as possible, spending too much time describing any research studies but use them to support your argument. In this way you are presenting an informed opinion.

■ ■ ■

Answer to question 7: candidate A

(a) The term secure attachment refers to being well attached to a caregiver and not being so frightened by strangers. The term insecure attachment is the opposite. A child that is insecurely attached might cry a lot when his or her parent leaves, and is not easily comforted.

e The first answer is muddled and basic but receives 1 mark because there is a glimmer of knowledge. The second doesn't quite make it to the full 3 marks because it covers some, but not sufficient, detail. (3 out of 6 marks)

(b) Bowlby's theory of attachment was that it was as important as vitamins are for physical development. Children become attached to a primary caregiver because it is an innate drive and without this attachment they will be emotionally maladjusted. You don't become attached because of spending time with another person but you become attached because the other person responds to your needs.

e The answer is badly constructed but displays a knowledge of several aspects of Bowlby's theory, making it better than muddled and flawed. Candidate A might have improved the answer by trying to offer an explanation rather than writing what he/she could remember about Bowlby's theory. (3 out of 6 marks)

(c) Studies of attachment in different cultures have shown that there are important variations. For example, Japanese children are more likely to be classed as anxious-resistant than American children. It is suggested that this is because of the way they are tested rather than because of their actual attachment type. The Strange Situation, which is used to assess how securely attached an infant is, presumes that infants the world over will react in the same way when they are left on their own by their mother. However, Japanese children are rarely left by their mothers and therefore they react to this fairly unusual situation by becoming very upset, while an American child is more used to this and therefore might appear to be more securely attached.

In other parts of the world, such as in parts of Central America, children are left alone in the dark for most of their first year of life because their society believes the world is a dirty place and children are best confined to the family home, and given very little attention. According to Western theories of attachment, this would result in maladjustment later in life because of a lack of early attachments. However, this doesn't seem to happen.

In a study in Israel it was found that the children were very attached to their mothers even though they didn't spend very much time with them. The children grew up in a children's home. But when they were tested the children were more securely attached to their mothers. This goes against the view that attachment is related to time spent together.

e This answer reads well and is focused on the question. A number of studies have been described and used to present relevant arguments. However, key details of the studies have been omitted (such as the researchers' names), which makes the evidence sound anecdotal, and thus this response is less detailed (4 out of 6 marks). The commentary is reasonably effective but somewhat limited in terms of what is discussed. The best points are made in the first paragraph; the remaining commentary is basic. Taken together, this gives 7 out of 12 marks for AO2, and a total of 11 out of 18 marks.

Total for this question: 17 out of 30 marks

Answer to question 7: candidate B

(a) Secure attachment refers to the strong and contented bond between an infant and its caregiver. It promotes healthy cognitive and emotional development and is probably the result of an interaction with a sensitive and responsive caregiver. There are various kinds of insecure attachment, such as avoidant attachment, which is shown by an infant who shows apparent indifference in the Strange Situation when the caregiver leaves. At reunion the infant actively avoids contact with the caregiver. This might result from insensitive caregiving. Other kinds are resistant attachment and disorganised attachment.

> Enough detail to award full marks for both answers (more than sufficient detail in the case of insecure attachment). (6 out of 6 marks)

(b) Bowlby proposed that attachment is adaptive — infants become attached to a caregiver because it promotes survival by ensuring safety and food for them. Infants are born with social releasers, such as crying and smiling, which elicit caregiving and thus ensure that others become attached to them. Bowlby insisted that attachment is reciprocal. The infant becomes attached to the person who responds most sensitively to his/her social releasers. One particularly important feature of Bowlby's theory was that attachments had to develop within a critical period or they wouldn't form at all. Bowlby said this had to happen by the age of $2\frac{1}{2}$.

> The candidate has written a well-detailed description of Bowlby's theory and as much as could be expected in 5–6 minutes. It is clear and accurate. (6 out of 6 marks)

(c) Different cultures around the world, and different sub-cultures within our own country, have different approaches to child-rearing. How do these different practices affect attachment?

Grossmann et al. (1985) studied attachment behaviour in Germany. Whereas in Britain about 75% of infants were classified as securely attached, using the Strange Situation, only 33% were classed as securely attached in Germany. It was suggested that the reason for this difference is that German parents value independence and self-reliance and would regard the behaviours that are taken to represent secure attachment as 'clinging'. Grossmann et al. observed the parents at home and found no evidence that they were insensitive or unresponsive, behaviours that have been linked to lack of attachment. Therefore we must conclude that the infants were probably attached to their parents but didn't express this in the same way as British children do.

A Dutch cross-cultural study compared rates of secure and insecure attachment worldwide and found some differences, but there were probably more similarities than differences. This is surprising given the fact that different cultures do have quite different childcare practices, as suggested above. It could be that some aspects of attachment behaviour are universal, as Bowlby suggested.

Aside from secure/insecure attachment, another cultural difference is in terms of multiple attachments. In our culture it is the norm for children to be brought up by just their parents, whereas in other cultures children often have an extended family. Bowlby felt that a child needs to establish a special bond with a primary caregiver for normal emotional development. There is little evidence from studies of other cultures that multiple bonding is harmful. It might benefit children to have variety in their relationships. On the other hand, there is evidence that even with multiple attachments children do still have a primary caregiver. For example, Tronick et al. (1992) studied a pygmy tribe in Zaire which lived in extended family groups. Infants and children were looked after by whoever was closest to hand. They were breastfed by different women but usually slept with their own mother. Tronick et al. found that, by the age of 6 months, the infants still did show a preference for their mothers — a single primary attachment. In addition, the study by Fox, of infant-rearing on a kibbutzim, showed that children remained more closely attached to their mothers despite spending more time with a metapelet.

This suggests that there are certain universals in attachment behaviour which remain, despite cultural variations in child-rearing.

The answer begins by focusing on what is required to respond to the question — this helps the candidate and the examiner to know what is expected. This is a good, well-organised attempt to address a difficult question mainly in terms of AO2 rather than AO1 skills. There is an obvious temptation to describe cross-cultural differences, whereas the question asks that you consider the extent to which such differences affect attachment behaviours. This candidate has struck a good balance between the two. There is an informed commentary which is reasonably thorough. This answer is worth full marks (18 out 18).

Total for this question: 30 out of 30 marks

Developmental psychology (IV)

(a) Describe *two* differences between 'deprivation' and 'privation'. (3 + 3 marks)

(b) Describe the aims and conclusions of *one* study of cross-cultural variations into attachment. (6 marks)

(c) 'For many years learning theory and psychodynamic theory dominated psychologists' understanding of the process of attachment. Bowlby's theory changed all this.'

Consider the extent to which explanations of attachment can account for the facts. (18 marks)

Total: 30 marks

(a) You should use your knowledge of these terms to work out two ways to distinguish between them. Each difference is worth 3 marks and therefore you must do more than just identify the difference: you must ensure that you explain the difference carefully, in order that your answer is described as detailed rather than limited or basic.

(b) Your answer need not be balanced between aims and conclusions, but you should ensure that both are covered, even if one is fairly brief. An 'aim' is what the researcher(s) intended to find out, i.e. their hypothesis. The conclusion is the sense that we can make out of the findings (it is not the same as the findings).

(c) The final part of the question requires some description of the 'facts' but twice as much evaluation and commentary. Take care to resist lengthy descriptions of any research evidence, though you might be tempted to fill the time with such material. When mentioning research evidence, you do not have to be able to name the studies and provide their dates, but it helps the examiner understand to what you are referring and provides important detail. Your discussion might include a consideration of the extent to which the 'facts' are definite. In other words, can we rely on the research evidence?

■ ■ ■

Answer to question 8: candidate A

(a) Deprivation is the loss of attachments while privation is a lack of attachments. It is suggested that only privation results in permanent long-term effects.

The first difference is correct and generally accurate for 2 marks, but there is not enough detail for 3 marks. In fact 2 marks might be rather generous, but we can balance this out with the second difference which is better than basic but not by much, so 2 marks for the first difference, and 1 for the second. (3 out of 6 marks)

(b) Ainsworth conducted a study of attachment in Uganda. The aim of this study was to observe differences in the infants' attachment behaviours. The conclusion was that there were three different kinds of attachment: securely attached, insecurely attached and not yet attached.

> *e* The candidate has focused, as required, on aims and conclusions, but details have been omitted. It could be that the candidate simply does not know any more details and perhaps this was not a good study to choose. (3 out of 6 marks — the description of both aims and conclusions lacks detail.)

(c) Bowlby's theory of attachment proposed that it is not feeding that makes a child become attached to an adult but that it is the kind of behaviour shown by the attachment figure. Learning theory suggests that infants become attached to the person who feeds them because feeding is rewarding and they learn to associate the reward with the person doing the feeding. Then the person doing the feeding becomes a secondary reinforcer. However, Harlow's research with monkeys showed that it wasn't food that was important, because the monkeys preferred to go to the wire mother who didn't have the feeding bottle. Harlow's study showed that it was contact comfort that was most important. However, it also showed that the monkeys grew up maladjusted because they didn't have mothers who interacted with them. We should be careful about generalising from this study to human behaviour.

Bowlby said that infants need to become attached; otherwise they suffer permanent emotional damage. They need a primary caregiver to act as an internal working model for adult relationships. If they don't have this model, or they don't have a secure relationship, they might find emotional relationships difficult in later life.

> *e* The candidate clearly has some knowledge about theories of attachment, as outlined in both paragraphs. However, the evidence presented here is somewhat limited in detail (4 out of 6 marks). Only one form of evaluation has been attempted in considering Harlow's research. A number of points are made in relation to this research and what it shows us, but the AO2 element remains rudimentary, for 4 out of 12 marks, making a total of 8 out of 18 marks.

Total for this question: 14 out of 30 marks

■ ■ ■

Answer to question 8: candidate B

(a) The term deprivation refers to a child who has been separated from an attachment object and experienced disruption of the attachment bonds. Privation occurs when there were no attachment bonds formed in the first place. A deprived child experiences loss of attachment, whereas the privated child experiences a complete lack of attachments.

Deprivation and privation also differ in terms of their consequences. Privation is associated with a greater likelihood of permanent effects on emotional development, whereas deprived children usually recover.

question

e Accurate and reasonably detailed for 2 marks each. Research examples would have been useful. (4 out of 6 marks)

(b) Van Ijzendoorn and Kroonenberg (1988) conducted a truly cross-cultural study by comparing the results from studies using the Strange Situation. The aim of this study was to see if different cultures (countries) had similar rates of attachment, and how much variation there was. They concluded that there was not much variation and that in fact there was as much variation within cultures as between cultures.

e Both aims and conclusions are covered and given in reasonable detail. The candidate might have been more specific about the aims and also provided some particular details about the conclusions (for example, secure attachment varied from 50% in China to 75% in Britain). (4 out of 6 marks — aims and conclusions are both described, and are generally accurate but limited.)

(c) Early theories of attachment, such as learning theory and psychodynamic theory, suggested that infants become attached to the person who feeds them. However, evidence from Harlow's study of monkeys showed very clearly that infants used a cloth-covered monkey model for comfort when they were frightened and spent most time with this 'mother' rather than the one with the feeding bottle. Perhaps even more importantly, the study showed that contact alone was not sufficient for healthy attachment because these monkeys were quite maladjusted. Schaffer and Emerson's study also found that an infant's primary attachment was not necessarily with the person who feeds them.

Bowlby's theory of attachment offered a way to explain why it is not feeding or time that is significant. According to Bowlby, infants become attached to the person who responds most sensitively to their needs.

Bowlby also said that the primary attachment relationship provides the infant with an internal working model about what relationships with others are like. If the infant can trust his/her mother (or whoever is the primary attachment object), then he/she can expect the same in future relationships. Clearly behaviourists would not accept such an explanation for attachment because they refuse to incorporate cognitive explanations into their theory. This shows that Bowlby altered the way we think about why attachment is important. He suggested how early attachment can affect later development.

Another change that Bowlby made was to introduce the evolutionary approach into our understanding of attachment. He argued that the reason infants become attached is because attachment is adaptive, in other words it promotes the survival of the infant and also of the parents' genetic line. Therefore this behaviour would be naturally selected.

e The candidate clearly has some useful and detailed knowledge about theories of attachment and two related studies. There is AO1 credit for the descriptions of the theories and some for the studies, though these descriptions are not always well detailed (5 out of 6 marks). AO2 credit is demonstrated by some effective use of the studies to consider whether the theory fits the facts and some further commentary on Bowlby's theory from the behaviourist standpoint and the value of his theory generally. The candidate has wisely interpreted some of the points (for example, 'This shows that…') to ensure that the question is being answered rather than simply presenting a description of Bowlby's theory of attachment (or the other theories). The scope of the analysis is somewhat limited, though reasonably effective, for 7 out of 12 marks, making a total of 12 out of 18 marks.

Total for this question: 20 out of 30 marks